I0027019

TRUMP ... Divine Intervention or Not?

How today's political shakeup is forcing all
Americans to see their own hypocrisy

Ce Ce Ferrari

Royal Python Press

Santa Ana, California

Royal Python Press
2781 W. MacArthur Blvd., #B259
Santa Ana, CA 92704

Ordering Information:
Quantity sales: Special discounts are available on quantity purchases by corporations, associations, and others. For details, contact the "Special Sales Department" at the address above.

ISBN: 978-0-996385-1-2-1

Acknowledgments

I am thankful and grateful for Rhonda Branch Yearby for her encouragement and for helping me to keep my light lit bright when it was dim, and for her publicity services, and helping to market me. I am thankful and grateful for Donna Weber for her editing services and for having integrity and completing the editing of my manuscript before the due date. I am thankful to Brian Bees for his professional, speedy completion of editing, and formatting my manuscript. I am thankful and grateful to Dormeka Pearce for fiercely managing my social media accounts. I am thankful and grateful to Timothy Madden for his encouragement, being a friend and a confidante. Timothy, your belief in me kept me writing this book.

Table of Contents

Preface

I wrote "Trump ... Divine Intervention or Not?" before the 2016 Presidential election. I am not a religious person, however during my prayers and mediations I was often told that Donald J. Trump would win the election. I often questioned this inner voice because Trump's poll numbers were consistently lower than Hillary's.

There were times when I was wakened during the wee hours to be told, "Donald J. Trump will be your next president."

I am a proud, black American woman who was a police officer. In this book, I share a unique perspective on Black Lives Matter, illegal immigration, personal responsibility and racism. I help the reader understand why I think Trump is a sheep wearing wolf's clothing.

Politically, I am Independent. Some of the best reviews I've gotten from this book are from Democrats because they appreciate my honesty. I don't defend or take sides just for the sake of political affiliation.

The racial divide in America isn't because of Trump being president. We have division within ourselves that we're refusing to see and heal. Trump is a giant mirror of who we all are. Some modern-day protesters come from goodness, however there are some who are protesting loudly in the streets under the guise of being "good" without doing their necessary internal work to become a better, authentic person.

I give many simple reasons as to why Hillary lost the 2016 Presidential election and why America needed a bold, bombastic leader like Trump.

I became a better person as a result of the 2016 Presidential election because I looked at the behavior of Trump and Hillary and I saw aspects of them within myself.

"Trump ... Divine Intervention or Not?" will trigger you to see the Trump *in* you.

I would love to hear your feedback after reading this book.

CeCeFerrari.com

"This book is informative and well written. It gives insight into why Trump won!"
—Mickey Howard

"Ce Ce's point of view on Trump's candidacy in the U.S. election is very interesting and enlightening, especially for a reader like myself that does not live in the USA. I really enjoyed her frankness and zest for being different from the masses."
—Peta

Chapter 1

An Escalator Ride Changed History

"**S**hut up! That little spicy mouth of yours is going to get you into trouble!" My mother often said those words to me, and sometimes I got spankings for saying things that were truthful but not so nice. One of Ma's Jehovah's Witness sisters was having problems with her husband and she spent some nights at our house. The woman slept in my bedroom and she snored like a broken lawnmower. After several hours of not being able to sleep, I yelled, "I can't sleep!" Ma quickly came into my bedroom and gave me a spanking. "How dare you hurt my sister's feelings!"

I was only a child, I felt confused because I was simply speaking the truth. I grew up being a Jehovah's Witness and Ma would remind me of how important it was to speak the truth and not lie. I later learned that I was to only speak the truth if my words were nice and didn't hurt anyone's feelings. Granted, religious people will quickly tell you, "You're going to hell," if you don't agree with their belief system. Telling people, they're going to die and burn in an eternal fiery furnace because they choose to worship different from your choice isn't being nice. Some religious people hide behind, "Well, that's what the Bible says."

On June 16, 2015, businessman Donald J. Trump glided down the escalator at Trump Towers and announced his run for the 2016 presidential election. Many thought Trump was a joke and felt he was announcing his run as a publicity stunt. I knew change was coming.

I am a fan of shock jock Howard Stern and Donald J. Trump because I admire their confidence to say controversial things and say what many are thinking. I relate to Donald Trump because I feel like the Trump of my family. I have grown comfortable with my voice. Sometimes when people don't want to hear certain things, there isn't a nice way to say what they don't want to hear. I am a member of Toastmasters International, an organization where you attend weekly meetings to improve your public speaking skills. At one of the meetings, I was asked an impromptu question in front of the group, "If you had to write a movie about presidents, what would your movie be about?"

"My movie would be about Donald Trump winning the 2016 presidential election." I felt a bouquet of emotions from the group. People are surprised when they find out I am a Trumpette—a female Trump supporter. Some were puzzled that I would be a Trump supporter because I am a black woman and I should automatically support a Democrat. After the meeting, a few people, Spanish, Asian and Caucasian, approached me and whispered that they, too, were supporters of Trump.

Politically, I am Independent. When it comes to women's rights, birth control, abortions and gay rights, I am liberal. I am conservative when it comes to taking responsibility for your personal behavior, creating success through education and living a life you can financially afford and not survive on welfare. I am not attached to one political party.

Trump quickly became more controversial when he said, "The U.S. is becoming a dumping ground for the world's problems. When Mexico sends its people, they're not sending their best. They're bringing drugs; they're bringing crime, they're rapists. And some, I assume are good people." He also said, "As many as 80% of female immigrants crossing the U.S. Mexico borders are sexually assaulted during their trip."

I was surprised with the media fury calling Trump's comments about what happens on the U.S. southern border hateful and racist. He simply spoke the truth about what happens on the border and in some communities. His words were refreshing to hear.

Chapter 2

Super-Predators

"Gangs of kids are 'super-predators' with no conscience, no empathy." These were the words spoken by Hillary Clinton in 1996 while speaking about black youth gang members. I wasn't offended when I heard this. I agreed with her. A predator isn't based on what race someone is. A predator is based on behavior. If people and gang members kill, assault, rape, rob and injure innocent people, then they are predators. I am not offended when the truth is spoken about black people. Instead of black people feeling offended by Hillary's assessment of a group of people who mainly kill and harm their own, they should've rallied behind her and put more effort into changing the behavior of the culprits doing the crime rather than bashing those who speak the truth about black people or any race of people who have poor behavior.

I was a police officer for the Miami Metro Dade Police Department. I personally dealt with super-predators on the streets. I saw generations on crime-ridden street corners hanging out using drugs and abusing alcohol. Sometimes, storefronts were lined with great-grandfather, grandfather, father and son.

I was disappointed with Hillary for apologizing for her super predator comment. Bill Clinton was speaking at a rally for Hillary in Philadelphia. Black Lives Matter protesters heckled him because of his multibillion-dollar crime bill from 1994 that funded more cops and prisons.

The bill had a mandated life sentence for three-time offenders. By the way, at the time Rep. Bernie Sanders also voted for the bill. Critics complained about the sentencing disparity for crack vs powder cocaine users because many upscale white people used cocaine. At a Hillary rally, a protester held up a sign that called her a murderer. Bill Clinton lost it and said, "I don't know how you would characterize the gang leaders who get 13-year-old kids hopped on crack and send them out on the street to murder other African American children. Maybe you thought they were good citizens, but she (Hillary) didn't. You are defending the people who kill the lives of who you say matter." I was proud Bill Clinton took a stand and spoke bold truth. Later, he said this about his exchange with Black Lives Matter, "I almost want to apologize." I was disappointed with his almost apology. He should've owned what he said because he was right on!

I have met some Mexicans who agree with what Trump said about Mexicans. The manner in which Trump spoke about the Mexicans may not be *pretty*, however he did speak the truth about a segment of Mexican people. I understand why some white people want to move out of their neighborhoods when black people, Hispanics and other minorities move into their neighborhoods. I also understand that not all black people and minorities disregard keeping their homes and yards maintained properly. I personally know African Americans and Hispanics who prefer not to live around their own people.

A neighbor who plays their music loud and keeps their living space dirty wouldn't be excused by me if they were white. It's the behavior that I wouldn't be happy with. If a white rocker was playing his heavy metal music loud I wouldn't give him a pass because his skin is white.

We've become an overly sensitive society as we

hide behind the politically correct police. Many underestimated Trump. I got his appeal right away because I have conversations with middle class and poor American citizens who are unhappy with our government because we think that there's more energy going toward helping illegal immigrants and refugees. The media spin is about calling Trump a bigot, bully and a racist. Trump may be bombastic; however, I think he's probably the least racist and the most authentic of the presidential candidates. Some say he speaks harshly. This may be true. I had a wise therapist who said that people like to focus on how something is said rather than focus on the message as an excuse to not embrace the messenger's message. Trump's comments have merit, and we need to have discussions about illegal immigration and Muslims entering our country. Demonizing Trump for the way he says things and not being willing to focus on the message doesn't help us grow as a nation and a world. Sure, I would say things differently than the way he says some things, however, I am attracted to his bold, provocative message. The truth isn't always pretty.

TRUMP ... Divine Intervention or Not?

Chapter 3

Black Lives Matter ... Really???

When I first heard the slogan "Black Lives Matter," I thought it was a phrase black people came up with to say to each other to help inspire black people to treat each other better. I found it comical that this slogan was meant for white people in order for them to stop mistreating black people. I was disappointed with President Obama for not publicly reprimanding Black Lives Matter and other protesters who chanted in the streets about police, "Pigs in a blanket, fry 'em like bacon!"

The black community needs the police more than any other community. By publicly saying they want cops harmed, they are hurting the very people whose lives they claim matter. Obama invited Black Lives Matter to the White House. Today, if you want an invitation to the White House it seems you have to have a sex tape that goes viral and become a reality star, or chant you want dead cops in the streets.

President Obama missed a grand opportunity by not publicly chastising Black Lives Matter for their behavior. A Black Lives Matter member went to a Bernie Sanders rally and snatched his microphone when he was speaking and she started speaking. Bernie had an outer appearance of calmness; his face turned tomato red, he was probably pissed off and was steaming inside. This was rude and disrespectful. If Bernie would've reprimanded her, he would've been called a racist. Trump said, "She wouldn't have taken my microphone!"

Black Lives Matter members have gone to other presidential rallies and created havoc. There have been Black Lives Matter members who have had physical confrontations with security and with white rally attendees at Trump rallies. It's a waste of energy to go to rallies and shout down presidential candidates from speaking. If Black Lives Matter members were smart, they would have requested civilized meetings with all of the presidential candidates and asked them what can they offer and promise them to improve conditions in black communities.

Some college Republicans, for National Police Week at Dartmouth College, posted slogans that said, "Blue Lives Matter." Black Lives members removed their posters and replaced them with their slogans saying, "Black Lives Matter." Employees removed the Black Lives Matter posters and replaced them with the original posters. Many of you probably didn't hear about this story. I bet you would've heard about it if the white students removed Black Lives Matter posters. The story would've been called, "Racism on today's college campuses."

Black Lives Matter members don't seem to be interested in bringing harmony and peace. Maybe they think they'll get more attention by being divisive. When I was a police officer and we felt like we were targets, we slowed down when answering violent calls in the hopes that most of the heat would've subsided by the time we arrived. When police officers feel like they're targets, there's more apathy and they care less about the people who need them the most.

Black Lives Matter members have hurt their own people more by publicly chanting they want police harmed. Crime in the black communities has increased. Less quality people want to be police officers as a result of Black Lives Matter wanting them dead, and this causes more problems with police and black people because they won't get the best police officers. Soon, the pool of potential police officers is going to be mainly thugs.

When I worked for the Miami Metro Dade Police Department, I could proudly say that the majority of men and women I worked with on the force were outstanding officers who took their oath to protect and serve as an honor. The saddest part is that usually it's the good cops who are randomly killed. By no means am I saying that all police interactions that end in violence or death are justified. Regardless of the officer's race, I feel the majority of police shootings aren't based on race. Sometimes, a video of a police interaction with a suspect doesn't show 100% of everything. There are times when a police officer has a split second to make a life-or-death decision.

I would love to see Black Lives Matter and other groups who are angry about white police officers killing black people take their protests into black communities, where black on black crime is high. I believe black protesters would truly care about black lives if they were consistently angry about anyone killing an innocent black person and not just getting in an uproar when a white person kills a black person.

I think there are a few reasons why some black people only protest when a white person takes a black life. It's painful to look at yourself and admit your own people are your biggest enemy. Black people get national media attention when they protest about white police officers who kill black men. Think about it, how many stories about black protesters protesting against black people killing black people have you seen on national television? Some black people get a false sense of superiority with the amount of media attention they get over protesting white police officers killing black people. When you have self-worth, high self-esteem and you truly care about innocent black lives being taken, you wouldn't give a damn about what race takes a black life.

Black Lives Matter should be on a mission to have more recruitment for blacks to become police officers, politicians, and become more involved with becoming members of our criminology and justice system. You create change from the inside out, and education and self-awareness are the best ways to get started with change.

I shouldn't be surprised that Obama aligned himself with Black Lives Matter, because he was a member of Reverend Wright's church for twenty years. Reverend Wright said America's chickens were coming home to roost after the attack on the World Trade Center in September 2001.

We need a president like Trump who would be bold enough to publicly call out Americans' poor behavior and say our country needs more law and order. Obama hasn't been a champion in helping to heal racial tensions in America. I think he gets off on racial tensions in our country because it helps him have a platform to speak about racist white Republicans.

Chapter 4

What Does Divinity have to do With Trump?

Most people are wolves in sheep clothing. I think Trump is a sheep wearing a wolf's clothing. He can be brash and bombastic; however, I think he's the most authentic of all the politicians running for the 2016 presidential election. Hillary is a wolf wearing sheep clothing. With The Donald, what you see is what you get.

Hillary is the biggest pimp of all the politicians! She'd look great with a grill of gold teeth, wearing a pimp daddy pantsuit with a fedora hat and feather glued to the side of it. She is probably the most disingenuous politician I've heard speak. She's no Bill Clinton. Bill is the reason I have an interest in politics. Years ago, I was watching the news and I saw a fine specimen of a man. "Who in the hell is that?" I asked. The television caption read, William Jefferson Clinton ... Governor of Arkansas. From that day on, I was sold on politics and I watched the news often to get a look at Bill and hear him speak.

Bill had a way of making you believe he was coming from the heart when he spoke publicly. I wasn't sure he spoke from his heart, however he convinced me he was. He had a way of making me feel warm inside. When he said his famous four words, "I feel your pain," I was a believer.

A news reporter asked a black man, "What is the best thing about Hillary Clinton?"

"Bill Clinton."

I so agree with that! There are millions of people who are still in love with Bill, and Hillary is their best way to still have a piece of him. Today, Bill has lost that spark. He seems brittle in mind and body and he doesn't seem to be at peace within. He's probably still pissed with the Republicans for bringing him down with the Monica Lewinsky scandal because he would probably have gone down in history as one of the best presidents.

Ronald Reagan and Bill Clinton were my favorite presidents because they seemed to have American pride. They spoke proudly about America and Americans. I didn't get that proud American feeling from President Obama. When giving a speech in France, Obama said Americans are arrogant and dismissive. It's rare you'll hear him speak about the atrocities some Muslim men commit against their women. Obama and the Democrats have been silent on the poor treatment of Muslim women in the Middle East. If Christians behaved the same as radical Islamic terrorists, many would blast them for such horrible behavior in the name of God.

Americans are also a very tolerant people. We put up with a lot because of the poor choices our politicians often make. The Democrats claim to care about poor people. However, lately Obama and many Democrats' concern has mainly been about refugees and illegal immigrants. Illegal immigration has made poor conditions in the black community worse. Our politicians' first obligation should be to the country's legal citizens.

When Trump stepped on the scene to run for the presidency, I knew something divine was happening. I think divine intervention is a part of everything in life. You can call divine intervention God, the universe or just natural cause and effect happening. I agree with what Trump said about the Mexicans on the border. I agree with what he said about Muslims entering the country. I think we should take it a step further and stop all immigration until we fix the holes in our Swiss cheese-like border situation.

Trump is in the race because divinity sent him to bring things back into balance. Trump isn't perfect; however, I love that he's forcing us to discuss issues we'd become comfortable burying. Necessary change isn't always pretty, and we're rocking and rolling right now on planet earth. Suppressing how we feel is more dangerous than Trump speaking boldly. We are being forced to change our ways and we've outgrown the need for the politically correct police. America, we've got some problems, and Trump is the least of them.

Divinity is forcing all of us to look inside of ourselves and be honest about our racist thoughts and beliefs, our discriminations, biases and our sexist ways. Every American and all humans are guilty of the above. He who says what he is *not* is often the very one with the most guilt.

Someone said, "Trump is going to get us into a war because of his mouth." Maybe other nations won't screw with us if we had Trump in the White House. I like that Trump is unpredictable. He's just what we need.

Mark Taylor is a fireman. In 2011, he was watching Trump on a television interview. While watching, he said he received a prophecy from God that Trump would become the President. He said Trump would help America be respected again and the American dollar would be strong again. This doesn't sound far-fetched to me. I think the biggest issue with Trump is that he could win the presidency and become one of the best presidents in history. Check out Mark Taylor's video on YouTube, it's interesting!

TRUMP ... Divine Intervention or Not?

Chapter 5

Pimp Momma Hillary to Illegal Immigrants: I Got Your Back

"**Y**ou can count on me to defend President Obama's executive actions on DACA (Deferred Action for Children Arrivals) and DAPA (Deferred Action for Parents of Americans and Lawful Permanent Residents) when I'm president," Hillary said. Her number one priority, should she win the election, is to give work permits and access to federal benefits to millions of illegal immigrants. She would allow millions of illegal immigrants to remain in America, receive work permits to legally fill American jobs and get access to federal benefits that are paid for by Americans. Her plan will give illegal immigrants full citizenship, which will give them welfare access, voting privileges and the ability to bring over their family members through chain migration. The Heritage Foundation said full amnesty will cost taxpayers $6.3 trillion.

Along with striving to give illegal immigrants amnesty during her first 100 days in office, Hillary said she would overhaul a nearly $300 billion infrastructure plan and make the biggest investment in good paying jobs since World War ll. Hillary said, "We need more jobs we can support a family on especially in places that have been left out and left behind." Apparently, Hillary doesn't care about American citizens who have been left behind in the work place as a result of illegal immigrants driving down wages. There are fewer jobs in America because of automation and the internet. What a time for Pimp Momma Hillary to make her number one concern illegal immigrants.

A couple of nights ago, while I was traveling cross-country, I was waiting at a gate in the airport for a flight when I met Martin, who is Mexican. CNN was on the television and as usual, they were discussing Trump.

"Me no like Trump," he said.

"Why?"

"Trump said all wetbacks need to go back to Mexico."

"That's not true," I said. "Trump didn't call Mexicans wetbacks."

"Yes, he did," Martin said angrily, nodding his head.

"I like Trump and I am voting for him."

"Really? You such a pretty, nice lady though. Why you like Trump?"

"I agree with what he says about illegal immigration. I think it's wonderful that America allows people from all over the world to come to our country, however I think people need to come here legally," I said. "Massive illegal immigration has forced wages to go down and many Americans have lost their jobs as a result."

"You know Miss Ce Ce; I tell you something, Trump is right. I have been in the United States since 1998. I was making $20.00 an hour in 2007 as a chef. My boss tell me, 'Martin, I have to let you go. I can get three employees for the price of one.'"

"Wow."

"Yes, my boss fire me and got three illegal immigrants for $7.00 an hour."

"I am an international lover and I love people with good character regardless of their race."

"I know you special, lady, that's why I sat by you."

"Most of my neighbors are Mexican," I said.

"Guess who is the favorite neighbor to the Mexican kids?'
"You?"
"Of course. They love me and they are beautiful children. When they see me they always yell, 'Hi Ce Ce,' and they run over to me."
"Very nice Miss Ce Ce, very nice," Martin said with a big smile on his face.

Martin and millions more like him aren't a concern for Pimp Momma Hillary because she wants to pimp Latinos for votes. Like many black people, Latinos think Democrats care about them. If they cared about them, they wouldn't encourage millions of poor people to enter our country illegally by rewarding their poor behavior by refusing to deport them and giving them welfare. It's shameful that our politicians are okay with piling millions of poor people into America at a time when millions of Americans are unemployed. If Democrats cared about poor Latinos and all races of poor people, they wouldn't be in agreement with massive illegal immigration because it causes more struggles for poor people.

The Democratic Party will mainly be responsible should America become a third world country and have devastating conditions like they have in Venezuela. McDonald's restaurant has discontinued selling Big Macs in Venezuela because they can't afford the third slice of bread that's in the center of the Big Mac. Because of hoarding, Venezuela's president wants to introduce finger printing for shoppers. When a store gets a shipment of corn flour, the word spreads on social media and hundreds try to get it. Many of the people don't have food on a daily basis.

Venezuela has the highest inflation rate at 180% and they have a shortage of basic goods along with having power shortages. Their reliance on imports worsens their situation. When politicians care about their people, they would ensure immigration laws that first protect the people they've given an oath to serve. Obama was right when he said illegal immigrants don't steal jobs away from us—they're given to them.

Whether our president is a Democrat or a Republican, their first priority for their first 100 days in office and beyond should always be about the welfare of legal citizens. Getting Kate Steinle's bill passed should be a priority now and for whomever becomes the next president. Steinle's bill would cut off federal funding to cities and states that have sanctuary cities that protect illegal immigrants, and those who are deported would get a mandatory five years in prison if they returned to the United States. I actually think Hillary knows what it takes to be a good politician; however, her pimping ways cloud her judgment. If she had integrity, she'd rather lose the election before she would sell out the American people.

When Hillary was first asked about how she felt about Juan Francisco Lopez (a.k.a. Jose Ines Garcia Zarate), the illegal immigrant who killed Kate Steinle on a pier in San Francisco, she said, "The city made a mistake, not to deport someone that the federal government strongly felt should be deported. I have absolutely no support for a city that ignores the strong evidence that should be acted on."

After making her wise comment, Hillary, being the pimp, she is, had someone from her campaign say, "Hillary Clinton believes that sanctuary cities can help further public safety and she has defended those policies going back years." What a sellout! I think Hillary is much more dangerous than Trump. At least Trump won't sell out the American people by supporting sanctuary cities that are filled with criminal illegal immigrants who get welfare from taxpayers. Crooked Hillary had to change her comment because she didn't want to piss off Latinos who took her comment to mean illegal immigrants should obey our immigration laws.

TRUMP ... Divine Intervention or Not?

Chapter 6

The New Racism

A black man got on an airplane on which a friend of mine was working. He asked a white male passenger, "Excuse me, would you mind changing your seat with me so I can sit with my wife?"

"No, I don't want to give up my aisle seat for a middle," the white man said.

"You see, I keep telling you, racism is alive and kicking," a black militant woman said to my friend.

"Is it possible he just didn't want to change his seat?" my friend asked.

"No, honey. I know how these crackers are."

I find it interesting that the same situations can happen to people of the same race. However, when another race (mainly white vs. black) is involved, the final analysis is automatically racism.

Many black women can attest to getting shitty treatment from black female beauticians. If we got the same poor treatment from white beauticians, you'd often hear about how racist white beauticians are to black women. The majority of black beauticians I've dealt with are ghetto fabulous. The worst kind of ghetto black person is one who thinks they're bourgeois (sophisticated).

It doesn't matter if the black beautician works from her home or a shop, their behavior is the same. I've had appointments and I've showed up to find no one at the shop or they wouldn't answer their home door. I got smart and purchased an emergency wig for these mishaps. Sometimes the black beauticians wouldn't speak to me when I entered their home or business. You can sit and wait for them for hours and they don't apologize. However, if you're fifteen minutes late they scold you. Their restrooms are usually filthy.

You have to listen to them yell at their kids. "Momma, can I have some Ramen noodles?"

"No. Boy you better get ya little black ass outta here!"

Sometimes I feel traumatized after a session with black beauticians. Where am I going with this? If we think white racists treat us so awfully, then we should make an effort to be gentle and treat each other with respect and honor.

Recently, I was blessed and found a black beautician whose name is Ke Ke. She is refreshing, professional and kind. I drive two hours to have a hair session with her.

All races are racist. I was watching the talk show "The View" during the time when actor Mel Gibson's ex-girlfriend released audio of him saying the word nigger. Whoopi Goldberg said she personally knows Mel and he's not a racist. She said, "I myself am a racist. Here's what happens if you cut me off while I'm driving and I happen to look over, whatever I see, that's what you are. You are a black (mumbling noise) or you are a white (mumbling noise) or you're a female (mumbling noise). You are everything in the book, and I realize given the criteria people are using for racist that I'm a racist." Some people went haywire over Whoopi defending Mel and said they've never called someone a racial expletive. I can honestly say I have! And you know, sometimes I may not verbally say it but I think it. I don't think someone is necessarily a better person because they haven't ever said nor had the thought that someone was a nigger or any other racial slur. Every black person I personally know has said something racist. Your ills may not be ills I commit.

From my hypnosis classes, I learned that I am either "on" or "off" for a word. The subconscious isn't analytical. Our minds may tell us when a certain race says a word we may or may not have an emotional charge. However, the truth is in the subconscious and not our conscious mind. Because my conscious mind tells me I am not offended by a word, that doesn't mean that I am offended by the word in my subconscious. I thought red was my favorite color, and while under hypnosis my subconscious revealed to me that my favorite color was blue.

If you think a word someone of a different race may call you is degrading, then I suggest you suspend calling yourself that word. Black people keep the word nigger alive by calling each other what they say is the most degrading word. Some white people and other races are confused by this. They don't understand why we call ourselves a degrading name. Rappers, along with many black people, keep the word alive and thriving. The word nigger is on an altar these days and can only be used by a select race.

As a writer, I want to have the right to use and speak words that any other person has the right to use. I don't think any words should be censored, because they all have their proper context. Black people think they have the copyright to the word nigger. Black people are the only race that I am aware of that gets off on calling themselves a word they claim is degrading; however, someone of another race is ridiculed for calling a black person a nigger. That says a lot about our lack of self-esteem, lack of self-love and lack of self-honor.

We glorify rappers and other artists who use the

word nigger. We don't bash or boycott radio stations, music labels and others who are responsible for helping their art sell with the usage of the word nigger.

Amber Rose is a beautiful woman who dated Kanye West. Every year she has the Slut Walk. I think it's cool for her to want to unite with young women and help them. However, it's important that we don't call ourselves names we wouldn't want certain people to call us. If I am okay with calling myself and my girlfriends a bitch, whore or slut, then I have to be okay with others calling me the same because I must be the example of how I want to be treated.

I think Trump is the least racist of all the 2016 presidential candidates. I think Trump takes people based on their merit and not their race. He seems to like hard workers who want to be successful.

I have a joke for you. What's the difference between a Democrat and a Republican? A Republican will call you a nigger to your face and a Democrat will call you a nigger behind your back. That's about the size of it, folks!

Chapter 7

Trump's Magic

People say some mean and nasty things about The Donald. He's a mystery. Had any other politician said the things he said in the era of political correctness, their chances of winning a primary or an election would've dried up. He knocked down 17 career politicians like he was a bowling ball making a perfect strike.

Many underestimate Trump. He's perceptive and he has the insight of an eagle. A Mafia Godfather said the best way to undermine your opponent is to know their weakness. Trump is a master at this. Calling Senator Ted Cruz "Lying Ted," Marco Rubio "Little Marco" and Jeb Bush "Low Energy Jeb," stuck to them like white on rice. Jeb Bush is a sleeper, and from the moment I saw Ted Cruz, I knew there was something distrustful and creepy about him. Before I heard anyone else say it, I thought Ted Cruz looked like Grandpa from The Munsters television show. I liked Ben Carson, but at times his motor skills seemed to be a bit sluggish. Carson is a brilliant man, however I felt the country needed a fireball like Trump.

I know how to decode what Trump says. I think many people who bash him also understand what he's saying. Instead of Trump being called a racist for speaking about the negatives of open borders and illegal immigration, Americans should agree with him that we should secure our borders and put the needs of American people first. Instead of calling him a racist, because of what he said about Muslims being banned from the United States until we can fix our immigration system, Americans should say they understand his focus is on keeping America safe. Yes, he could've spoken about illegal immigration and Muslims entering the United States in a more diplomatic way.

A black Muslim woman asked me, "Trump is a racist, how can you support him? You're so nice."

"What did he say or do that's racist?"

"He wants to ban Muslims from the U.S."

"I think our government should go farther and cease all immigration to the U.S. until we fix our broken system," I said. "I understand why Trump said what he said about Muslims."

"What do you mean?"

"Of course, we have wacky people of all races and religions who want to kill and blow people and structures up, however, Islamic radicals have an agenda to take over the entire world and force everyone to become Muslims."

"I agree with the terrorists," the Muslim woman said. "I hate white people because they're rich."

"You may hate white people, but I bet most of your troubles have come from black people," I said. "Not all white people are rich. Have you watched Jerry Springer?

"I get jealous because it seems like other people are happy and I'm not."

"Sister, you've got some *you* problems just as I have some *me* problems. I was poor because I made poor choices."

"I made some poor choices alright. My son is in prison for selling drugs and he got shot five times."

"Many of us have made some poor baby daddy choices. The white man didn't twist our arms to lay down with losers," I said. "You know we black people are our own worst enemies."

"You're right about that. In my family, they play favoritism if your skin is light, and if you're dark-skinned, you get treated like a stepchild," she said.

"Black people have so many issues within, individually, as a family and as a community. If we focused on our own issues, we'd forget racism exists because we'd be busy focusing on our own crap."

"I'm hearing a lot of black people say they're voting for Trump.

"I'm voting for Trump because I think it's time we have a president that's nice to legal American citizens."

Trump's magic dwindled for a minute when he retweeted a picture of his attractive wife Melania, next to an unflattering picture of Ted Cruz's wife, Heidi. When I saw that, I said, "Ouch!"

I knew that photo would anger women. Many women are insecure about their appearance, even if you may think they're attractive. Some women identified with Heidi Cruz, and to them Trump said they weren't attractive either. After that, his approval numbers with women took a dip and he lost the Wisconsin primary that he was once favored to win.

Leave it to the magical Trump, he bounced back from the Heidi Cruz photo controversy and went on to win more delegates.

For this reason, I agree with Trump about having a temporary ban on Muslims entering the country. If there's someone with a specific, unique talent that the U.S. needs, then I think we should make exceptions for immigration to the U.S. However, we're in overload already with millions of poor immigrants who are getting government assistance.

If there were radical Christians who were killing and bombing people because they didn't want to be Christians, I think more modern-day Christians would speak up and say they disagree with the radical

Christians' behavior. Most peaceful, nice Muslims are quiet about the behavior of radical Islamic terrorists. I found this to be true after the September 11, 2001 terrorist attack. I think that one-day Muslims will take over the world. If a worldwide Jihad was called, whose side do you think the so-called peaceful Muslims would take? A unified Jihad will be easier as Muslim refugees spread all over the world. There may come a day in America when Democrat and Republican women will be forced to wear burkas. Trump is shaking things up with what he's saying and the style in which he speaks. Rather than using energy to call Trump names, we should have discussions about what he's bringing to our attention. Trump is right on about many things, and two percent of Muslims plan to vote for him.

Chapter 8

The New Legal Illegal Immigrant

"**V**aledictorian, 4.5 GPA, full tuition paid for at UT (University of Texas), 13 cords medals, nice legs, oh and I'm undocumented." Mayte Lara, an illegal immigrant posted this on Twitter. Thousands of legal American citizens were angry with Mayte's arrogant disrespectful tweet and they let her know it on Twitter. She closed her account because she got such a backlash. She probably wasn't expecting this kind of response from Americans because she, like millions of other illegal immigrants, knows that the politically correct police and politicians have muzzled American citizens for speaking out against illegal immigration. Many Americans pride themselves on being good people, and they don't like being called bigots and racists.

Many illegal immigrants have Mayte's ungrateful attitude. If Americans were in other countries illegally and they publicly did the same, there would be worldwide news about the arrogant Americans! Illegal immigrants can afford to boldly shove their illegal status into the face of Americans because they have pimping politicians who reward them for violating American immigration laws. To make it worse, there are politicians who will call American citizens racist for not condoning people entering the United States illegally.

How did this happen, Americans? People cross the border illegally and overstay their visas and the American citizen becomes the anti-Christ for calling them out.

When illegal immigrants hear presidents and politicians say they should get to remain in the country and get legal status, they hear a call to come to America in droves. When a politician gives them a stamp of approval for being in our country illegally, they have the balls to give Americans who disapprove of them entering the country illegally their middle finger.

Mayte probably wouldn't have gotten the negative backlash she got if Donald J. Trump hadn't entered the 2016 presidential race. Trump gave millions of Americans their voice back. Millions of Americans are suffering and I think that too many of our politicians seem to have the interest of illegal immigrants and refugees as their first priority. Many Americans fought for years to have an end put to illegal immigration. When the voices of those calling us, racists got louder than our voices to send illegal immigrants back home, we quieted ... until the rise of Trump!

It's disheartening to be called a racist because I am for having secured borders and having people deported who are in our country illegally. If we don't deport illegal immigrants, then there's an invitation for millions more to enter the country illegally. I've heard Mexicans in the media say Americans are racists because we want people to enter our country legally. However, they fail to quote the strict, harsh immigration laws of Mexico. It's illegal to be in Mexico illegally, and you're not allowed in Mexico if you're a criminal. You have to sustain yourself economically and not be a burden on their society. It's a felony to enter Mexico illegally and they deport more than the United States government deports.

It's a misdemeanor to enter the United States illegally. You can be fined up to $250 and receive up to six months in jail. In Mexico, it's a felony to enter their country illegally and you can get up to ten years in prison for re-entering. Trump wants to build a wall. The best wall would be E-verify. E-verify is an internet-based system that compares info from Form I-9, Employment Eligibility Verification to Department of Homeland Security (DHS), Social Security Administration (SSA) and Department of State (DOS) records to confirm you are authorized to work in the United States. For years, Democrats and some Republicans have voted down bills to make E-verify a law because it would punish companies and charge them large fees for hiring illegal immigrants. I wonder why?

United States law requires companies to employ only individuals who may legally work in the United States, i.e. citizens or foreign citizens who have the necessary authorization. Based on this information, we have many politicians who are ensuring that our laws aren't being enforced. Most Democrat politicians don't want immigration bills that include E-verify. Democrats and Republicans have interest in illegal immigrants remaining in America. The Democrats pimp them to remain in office, and Republicans like them for cheap labor.

You may say, "But illegal immigrants can't vote." Because our presidential election is based on the Electoral College vote and not a popular vote, illegal immigrants play a role because delegates are based on the number of people in a district that are given in the United States Census. A politician is given a certain number of electoral votes based on the number of people in each state. There's one vote for each member in the House of Representatives plus two for senators.

Are you starting to get it? Yes, illegal immigrants are very important to the outcome of presidential elections. Democrats are on a mission to allow as many illegal immigrants into our country with the hopes they will mainly live in districts that are heavily Democrat. We have politicians selling out the American people for the sake of remaining in office as long as they possibly can. Of course, Trump and his bold, blunt, right-in-your-face style of speaking appealed to millions of Americans. Trump made millions of Americans think, "American Lives Matter." In 2014, the United States Department of Labor certified a record number of 116,689 seasonal employees picked crops in America. If we need less than 120,000 people to pick crops, then you must be wondering what jobs the other eleven million-plus illegal immigrants in America are doing.

Chapter 9

Hey, Where's My Free Section 8 Housing???

When I hear politicians say we need a new comprehensive immigration bill that will bring illegal immigrants out of the shadows, I laugh. I say illegal immigrants; however some politicians call them undocumented. They're undocumented because they're in the country illegally. That's like calling a street drug dealer an unlicensed medicine distributor.

If you boldly protest in the streets demanding legal status, toting signs that say, "Illegal, so what?" and "Fuck America," and carry Mexican flags right side up and carry the American flag upside down and burn American flags in daylight, then you aren't in the shadows. If you go to the DMV and apply for driver's licenses, you aren't in the shadows. If you are in the country illegally and you apply for food stamps, you aren't in the shadows. If you have several babies you can't afford and have them delivered for free at American hospitals, you aren't in the shadows.

You are definitely not in the shadows if you're in the country illegally and you are getting government welfare and are living in Section 8 housing for free or for a minimal cost when millions of Americans are struggling to pay their bills. The bright sunshine is shining on you. Check this out: In some states they don't even ask you about your legal residence status. America is an awesome deal for illegal immigrants. They can come and get benefits and if American citizens complain about it, they're called racists and the illegal immigrants get sympathy.

I have neighbors who are in the country illegally who get welfare. I don't think I am a racist because I am unhappy about that. I've had two pay cuts on my job; however, I don't qualify for government assistance. There are millions of Americans who are struggling, along with many of our veterans. Our veterans should be the number one group who our government is focused on helping. There are some Americans who could care less about helping our veterans. However, they're all for paying higher taxes to support illegal immigrants.

According to ModernHealthcare.com a vaginal baby delivery can cost $18,328 and $27,866 for a C-section baby delivery. Many illegal immigrants aren't paying for the births of their babies who automatically become anchor babies and get automatic citizenship. We, the American taxpayers, are footing the bill. This is one of the reasons insurance and hospital costs are high. I know illegal immigrants who are on government assistance and they are on baby number five who will also get citizenship, welfare and free school lunches. Why am I called a racist for not supporting our politicians for condoning this? We already have enough irresponsible Americans who do the same.

Mexicans aren't the only people in our country illegally. There are people from all over the world who are in America illegally. It doesn't matter to me what country people are from when they are in the country illegally. I don't care if they are from Zimbabwe. Our politicians encourage and reward poor behavior by awarding amnesty to people coming to our country illegally or remaining in our country with expired visas. Americans should be the priority for our politicians.

I am not a racist. I had to work on not allowing others to cause me to feel angry because they called me a racist for wanting our borders secure and for wanting strict immigration laws. I live in an apartment complex in California. The manager told me I am paying $500 more for rent because of supply and demand. If there weren't millions of illegal immigrants in the United States, there would be more affordable properties, and poor people and the middle class wouldn't have to pay as much for housing.

Allowing open borders and not deporting illegal immigrants is helping them improve their living conditions, however the rich aren't the ones suffering. The poor and the middle class are getting the short end of the stick because of mass illegal immigration. I think one of the beauties in America is people from all over the world are allowed to migrate to our great nation legally.

The DMV is always packed in California. There are just too many people! The DMV has been run poorly for years, and with the influx of millions of illegal immigrants the service is worse. The employees are burned out from the beginning of their work day. It's just too much! Because of millions of illegal immigrants being in California and going to the DMV, you can't physically go to the DMV to get your renewed registration because the office staff is overwhelmed. Your registration has to be done by mail now unless your registration has expired. I don't appreciate not having the option to go into the DMV office to purchase my registration. I think I am being penalized because of millions of people who shouldn't be in America. Legal citizens are being punished so our politicians can pimp votes.

Wealthy politicians and others call Americans racist for not being happy about millions of illegal immigrants being in our country. Poor illegal immigrants set up shop in mainly poor black neighborhoods and other poor neighborhoods. Maybe if poor refugees and illegal immigrants moved into some of the wealthy politicians' communities and crime increased, they would understand how many Americans feel. It's easy to say how others should think and feel when you're looking down from your fancy house on the hill.

I was surprised to hear President Obama be supportive of illegal immigration, because he should know more than anyone that the black communities suffer the most as a result of mass illegal immigration. I have spoken to inner city school teachers, and they say the public schools are a mess because they've had to abandon programs that were helping illiterate black students raise their literacy levels and teach illegal immigrant children instead. Crowded classrooms and defunding programs that once helped black children has resulted in more black children still speaking Ebonics.

Black teenagers have a high rate of unemployment because illegal immigrant adults are doing many of the jobs the black youths were once able to hold in their neighborhoods. Illegal immigration causes more crime, along with causing the cost of housing to increase. It's shocking the amount of money some poor black people are paying for rent and housing in ghetto-trapped neighborhoods. Again, this has to do with supply and demand. They have to share housing with millions of illegal immigrants. Black people have the strongest voice against massive illegal immigration, however they save their energy to only protest when white police officers kill black people.

Some black people have told me that they can't get hired in restaurants because Mexican managers won't hire them because they only hire Mexicans. Politicians shouldn't be part of the aggravation of an already horrible situation for their citizens. President Obama has spoken more about helping illegal immigrants and refugees than he has for black Americans. By no means do I think Obama should only be the president for black people;

however, he should've thrown the black community a bone every now and then.

During the 2016 presidential state of the union address, Obama said immigrants don't take jobs away from Americans. That was a big fat lie! When people say, "Illegal immigrants are doing the jobs Americans don't want to do," I say, "Illegal immigrants are doing work Americans don't want to do for minimum wage." In the eighties, my black male relatives had a difficult time getting work in the construction business because white men were dominating the jobs because they were being paid $20 to $25 an hour. With massive illegal immigration, Mexicans started doing construction work for $7 an hour. In the nineties, Americans, black, white, Asians, Latinos and others cleaned airplanes and they got decent salaries with benefits. Now airplane cleaners get $8 an hour without benefits. American white males used to dominate driving semi-trucks long distance. Many Mexicans now drive trucks for $10 an hour. By the way, it's disingenuous for politicians and others to accuse Trump of being racist when they speak about immigrants when they know he's speaking about "illegal immigrants."

Liberals who claim to love poor people should be aware that illegal immigration and open borders harm poor American citizens. Some liberals seem to only care about foreign poor people and not give a damn about poor Americans. The majority of problems in America that liberals are angry about have to do with illegal immigration. Liberals and many Americans are unhappy about low wages. Americans don't have the leverage they used to have as workers because there are millions of illegal immigrants who are waiting to get their jobs, sometimes for more than 60% less pay. Americans are upset about the high cost of housing and rent, which is also due to millions of illegal immigrants needing housing, and there are fewer affordable houses and apartments being built today. Americans are concerned about more crime. Illegal immigrants have brought more crime to America. Poor Americans are concerned about high medical costs; illegal immigrants have increased the cost of health care because taxpayers are paying for many of them to have health care.

Americans are unhappy about crowded neighborhoods and highways. Illegal immigrants cause our streets to be jam packed. I vividly remember when illegal immigrants had one of their protests to demand amnesty. I was driving on the 405 Freeway in Los Angeles in rush hour traffic and I was able to drive 70 mph. This is unheard of during this time of day. It was because thousands of illegal immigrants were at their protest. I was listening to talk radio and there were many Americans excited to have their highways back. They were saying they wish the illegal immigrants would protest this way every day. People were honking their horns with excitement. We got to see why our freeways were often jam-packed. The Mexicans' plan was to shut down businesses because they went to the protest instead of going to work. Americans can survive and be healthier with fewer fast food restaurants.

The conditions in poor black communities and other poor communities drag the system down, and I think it's important for our politicians to institute programs that will give poor people more opportunities. I actually think there's too much giving in America and not enough lifting by granting opportunities. Some black people say, "But, everything good Obama tried to do, the Republicans stopped him."

"What programs did Obama create that would give black people better opportunities, and better paying jobs that the Republicans stopped him from creating? None." I don't get an answer when I ask this question. Here's the deal, people: according to Census.gov, black people are

13% of the population and Hispanics are 17% of the population. Obama may be a black man; however, he is a politician and he too pandered to where he could get the most votes. Black brothers and sisters, you weren't a priority to the black president, nor the white presidents. Black people need to be more like Jewish people. Jews were discriminated against, so they banded together and looked out for each other and didn't wait and depend on the government. Because a politician is of a certain political affiliation, race or gender doesn't mean they have your best interest at heart.

Some black people don't like that I speak negatively about our black president or black people. I speak positively and negatively about all races and genders of people. I am an independent writer/author/speaker and it's important that I am authentic and speak my truths as I see it. A black person said to me, "I don't speak badly about black people to white people."

"I do. It's not like white people don't see black people on the news," I said. If my child, parents, lover or friends behave poorly I will call them out.

If Trump wasn't part of the 2016 presidential election, I doubt we would be discussing illegal immigration. Bernie Sanders said the collapse of Wall Street hurt the black community more than any other group. What he didn't say was that illegal immigration hurt the black community more than any other group. He didn't say this because he, too, was pandering to Latinos but because he wants to pad America with illegal immigrants in Democratic districts. Hillary dodges speaking about the negatives of illegal immigration but grandstands and says Trump doesn't like immigrants. She intentionally won't say, "Illegal immigrants." The Anchor Baby Program, that gives illegal immigrant people automatic citizenship if they're born in America is a joke for modern times.

I am interested in programs where one person gets help and they pass the baton by helping the next person become healthy and responsible. I've heard stories about rich and famous people helping poor people get new homes after weather tragedies. I am for this kind of help. However, I am not into just giving people the house for free. The people I would help would have to be part of the building process of their home, and then they would pass the baton and help someone else in need either by helping them rebuild their home or life. This way, people think they have a purpose and they become part of the end result rather than someone handing them the end result. This also builds self-worth and self-esteem and helps people feel valued.

Chapter 10

Walmart Gone Wild

Television shows like "Cops" and "Jerry Springer" are reminders that niggers come in all races. I think it's important for ethnic people to understand why people sometimes feel and think the way they do about certain races. Stereotypes exist because we the people keep them alive. I don't think it should be politically incorrect to discuss stereotypes. There is something to descriptions about some group behaviors. The danger with stereotyping is when we think people are 100% a certain way. Paying attention to stereotypes can help us understand why people think and behave the way they do, and we can see how you can get stuck in your growth when you only associate with a group who have a one thought/one mind reality.

There was a time when Mexicans were my favorite foreigners. I liked them because they seemed proud to be in America. Many of today's Mexicans who are illegal immigrants have an entitlement attitude and a "fuck you America" attitude. I think this attitude became rampant when politicians reprimanded Americans for not being happy about the many negative effects illegal immigration has brought to our cities and communities. Illegal immigrants felt empowered observing American citizens being called racists for being angry about seeing their great nation getting worse, not better.

Obama, the chief executive of the United States government led the case to give eleven million or more illegal immigrants amnesty. This caused many illegal immigrants to get cocky and arrogant. President Bush started it, and many politicians co-signed onto this poor behavior. The politicians not supporting deportation and supporting amnesty caused more illegal immigrants to enter America.

Again, Mexicans aren't the only illegal immigrants in America. People often ask me why people single out Mexicans when they speak about illegal immigrants. I will tell you why I think this is so. Black Americans and Latinos are usually the people the world sees on television news when stories are about crime. There seems to be more crime in poor black and Latino communities. Black women (thank goodness!) have slowed down on the number of children they have. Mexican women seem to be the group in America who procreate the most. It's common to see a Mexican woman with a baby in her belly while four more children are following her. There are many Asians in America illegally, however they stay under the radar and it's rare you see them with a lot of children on bus benches. Asians and other races who are in America illegally seem to be more educated and their neighborhoods are cleaner. We don't hear about them killing each other at the rate blacks and Latinos kill each other.

There was a Home Town Buffet restaurant I used to enjoy going to. With the influx of illegal immigrants, they would eat there, too. I don't have an issue with the race of anyone. I have a problem with poor behavior. The Mexican children would put their hands in the foods that were out for the buffet and their parents wouldn't say anything. There were salad greens in the beans and meat in the fruit bowl and food was on the floor. The last time I was there I was with my niece and she vomited after watching the Mexican kids stir the buffet foods with their fingers. I haven't eaten at a Home Town Buffet since. I've heard several people have the same complaint.

Black mothers are the best when it comes to chastising their misbehaved children in public. I was at a Walmart store where a lot of illegal immigrants shopped. It was insane trying to maneuver around in the store because the Mexican children ran through the store screaming and knocking over racks of clothes, and their parents wouldn't say a word. I felt like I was playing dodge ball to keep them from running into me. Someone from customer service got on the PA system and said, "Parents, please, please contain your children. They are not allowed to run in the store." The announcement was also made in Spanish; however, their behavior didn't change. The Walmart stores where Mexicans shop are often dirty and untidy. If I have to go to a Walmart, I make an effort to go to one in a better neighborhood. I like the deals you find at Marshalls and Ross stores. However, the ones where Mexicans shop are messy and the children behave the same way they behave in some Walmart stores. Not all Mexicans behave poorly. I also avoid some places where black people shop because the stores are poorly maintained and are often dirty.

One day I went to the DMV. I was sitting next to a Mexican family. The toddler son chewed gum and then spread it on the seat of the chair. The parents watched him and didn't say a word. A white woman finally said, "Stop that!" The parents didn't utter a word and the toddler continued to spread gum on the chair. The white lady and I shook our heads at each other. I was angry sitting in the overstuffed DMV for hours. Before massive illegal immigration, I would've been done in less than thirty minutes. My anger didn't have anything to do with the race of the people causing the jam at the DMV. It was the behavior of the child and the overcrowded situation I was unhappy about. All I could think about was how our politicians have screwed over the American people.

These are just a few incidents I have experienced with Mexicans and other races of people who are illegal immigrants. Of course, we've always had Americans who have this same kind of behavior; however, these kinds of conditions and behaviors escalated when millions of illegal immigrants from third world countries entered America. It's understandable why people from a third world country behave this way because it's their way of life. What's troubling is that our politicians don't consider the welfare of Americans when they allow millions of illegal immigrants to flood our country.

Sometimes, illegal immigrants from South America behave the same way. We have illegal immigrants from many countries, however illegal immigrants from Mexico and people from South America seem to have this kind of behavior the most. Regardless of what someone's race is, I feel more inconvenienced when the behavior is poor by people who shouldn't be in America. I am black and I am not offended when I hear about white people who don't want to live in neighborhoods with black people and Latinos. This doesn't mean all black people and Latinos are dangerous to live around, and they don't all have poor upkeep of their properties. I don't care if my neighbors are black, white, Asian, Latino, gay, straight, transgender, or bisexual. My concern is having clean, respectable neighbors. However, I know black people and Latinos who want to avoid living in communities with some of their own people.

I live in a complex that is mainly Mexican. The landscape on the property is beautiful and it looks like a resort with waterfalls. When the leasing agent showed me the unit that's near the pool, I asked her if it's always quiet because I need a quiet space to write in. The leasing agent assured me the property was always quiet. For some reason, I happened to be visiting the complex on one of the few times the complex was quiet. Well, let me tell you, this is the loudest complex I've ever lived at. The Mexican children scream for hours. They scream at the top of their lungs and then they jump in the pool. They scream while in the water for hours. Sometimes I get a headache from the screaming. There's a white woman who is my neighbor who asked me, "Is it a cultural thing with the way they scream?" I know all children scream, however I've never experienced this level of screaming before. Then, I have to listen to the loud boom-ditty-boom-boom music!

I have complained to the manager, but they don't care because most of the residents don't care about having a quiet, civilized community. The residents behave poorly in a complex where I am paying over $500 more than what the unit is worth because of illegal immigration and politicians who sold me out. Sometimes, the residents don't put their garbage in the garbage bin. They set it down next to the bin. Again, these behaviors can be done by all races, however I do tend to notice this behavior with blacks and Latinos. I know there are white communities where the same happens. I am giving you reasons why people seem to single out Mexicans when they complain about illegal immigrants. When most people think about criminals, they think about black people and Latinos because our groups seem to commit more crimes. I am not saying this is right; I am just giving you reasons as to why some people may think as they do. There are many black people and Latino people who would feel the same way about their people if they were white. It's about understanding.

I have been blessed to have met quality people from all races who are good people. I am open to dating any race man if he has good character.

Maybe the government can review each case uniquely when it comes to what should be done about illegal immigrants. At the same time, I don't think Trump is racist for saying illegal immigrants should be deported. Illegal immigrants who are criminals should definitely be deported whether they have anchor baby children or not. I find it interesting that Trump is the boogeyman for wanting illegal immigrants deported, while the illegal immigrant is held in high regard for entering our country illegally. Trump has been accused of breaking up families because he wants illegal immigrants deported. Illegal immigrant parents are responsible for their choice to enter America illegally and they don't have to break up their families. They can return to their countries and take their children with them. If their native countries won't allow them to take their anchor baby children back to their country, the government should have sanctions in place for those countries.

Thank goodness, the Supreme Court blocked Obama's executive order to give five million children of illegal immigrant children legal status. These children aren't anchor babies; they were born in countries where their parents migrated from. Children sometimes have to suffer because of the sins of their parents. There are many Americans who have sympathy for illegal immigrants and think it's okay for them to cause poor conditions for Americans because they are human too and we shouldn't have secure borders. These same people would like to lock the doors to their homes and not have to allow strangers to enter just because they're in need. These bleeding-heart Americans wouldn't want to be responsible for feeding people other than their immediate family every day at their dinner table. I am about having compassion and helping poor people, but the help shouldn't be a detriment to legal citizens.

Obama said, "For more than two decades, our immigration system has been broken." He's correct. It's broken because our politicians refuse to enforce our immigration laws and they aren't interested in deporting illegal immigrants as they enter America. When illegal immigrants apply for welfare, they should get temporary assistance while their process for deportation begins. A comprehensive immigration law means amnesty to me. I have personally spoken to people from all over the world who have been trying to get to America the legal way, yet our politicians reward people who enter the country illegally and put people who are following the legal process to the back of the line. Some ask, "Should I go to Mexico and cross the border illegally in order to get to stay in America?"

Obama and many politicians want to make America browner because they are banking on brown people voting Democrat, and this will enable them to have lifetime political appointments. The race and the skin of a human doesn't dictate their character. Just because people entering the country illegally are mainly brown doesn't mean we are getting the best of immigrants entering America. Some legal and illegal immigrants don't respect America and they aren't here to assimilate and be honest citizens. Many cause Americans and their own people harm.

I've also noticed a decline in the quality of work we get from illegal immigrants. Just because someone is in the country illegally doesn't mean that they haven't taken on the entitlement mentality that many millennials have. Legal and illegal immigrants don't have the gratitude and pride to be in America the way I noticed many had in the eighties and nineties. Like Americans, many of them are lazy. There was a time when you got a better deal by hiring illegal immigrants for construction work, cabinet building, maid work and landscaping. I hear many Americans say their rates have gotten higher and the quality of work has decreased.

I got tired of going to fast food restaurants and the non-English speakers would get my order wrong. I ordered a Whopper and I got home and realized I had a fish sandwich. One time I went to Wendy's and ordered a chicken salad. When I got home, I saw just a bowl of lettuce. More than ever, you have to check your food order before you leave. Today, many illegal immigrants are protesting to get $15 an hour to work at fast food restaurants. Whenever we the people do things out of greed, it will eventually backfire on us. For years, companies were happy to replace American workers with lowly paid illegal immigrants. This has come back to bite employers in the butt! It would've been smarter to pay Americans decent salaries, and then we wouldn't have millions of illegal immigrants crowding our freeways, raising the cost of healthcare and increasing crime.

One illegal immigrant who kills an American is one too many to be in our country. It's shameful how some of our politicians reward illegal immigrants' poor behavior.

Some Americans aren't aware that there are some jobs that illegal immigrants can't have because they don't have legal status. When millions of illegal immigrants get legal status, they will compete with millions of unemployed American citizens who have been suffering due to the downturn in the economy. Illegal immigrants aren't allowed to work for airlines, and they aren't supposed to work for our government. However, in 2007, there were two illegal immigrants who were appointed to government positions in Huntington Park, California. One was appointed to the Parks and Recreation Commission and the other held a position with the Health and Education Commission. Illegal immigrants shouldn't be allowed to run for office. These appointments caused an uproar in California.

When illegal immigrants were coming in droves in

the early nineties to America, white people weren't saying anything because they were mainly going into poor black neighborhoods. When illegal immigrants started to penetrate white neighborhoods, protests started because they knew the conditions in their communities would decline, and they have. In some neighborhoods, where parking wasn't assigned, street parking became a major issue because some illegal immigrants would have several adults living in one unit. If most of them had cars, this meant more cars were parking on the street and Americans were having difficulty finding street parking. Americans were frustrated because their livelihood was changing while being called racists for not being happy about the demise of their neighborhoods.

Thank goodness, we have Trump, who wants to enforce our immigration laws. It's a poor excuse to say, "People come to this country illegally because the immigration process takes too long." I don't think this is a reason to enter someone's country illegally. I think our politicians bear most of the responsibility for millions of illegal immigrants being in our country because they refuse to enforce our immigration laws and illegal immigrants know they want them here.

How can Hillary say Trump doesn't know anything about national security when she refuses to address the illegal immigration issue? It's a national security issue to have open borders. If you're weak on national security, then you're also a poor leader with international security and policy. Rather than calling Trump a racist for wanting to deport millions of illegal immigrants, politicians should be embarrassed to publicly say there are eleven million or more illegal immigrants in America, because this is confirmation that they haven't done their job to protect Americans' safety, jobs and welfare.

When I visit Asia, I miss the diversity we have in America. Immigration is a beautiful thing when it's done properly. Our politicians remind me of a man who is married and has three children. The married man takes care of his mistress and her children first, and the money he has left over he shares with his family. The husband's first obligation should be to his wife and children just as our politicians should put the American people first. After Americans' needs have been taken care of, then it will be a nice gesture to welcome foreigners to come to America legally. Today, the legal American is the underdog. There was a time when Americans felt comfortable to openly say foreigners who live in America should learn to speak English. If you say that today, you're called a racist. I am about change. However, people migrating to America should make it a better country, not worse. Illegal immigration has caused more harm than good.

I've met Latinos who are in America legally who complain about the poor conditions illegal immigration has brought to their communities and lives. Australia has stopped immigration to their country because they want to ensure their citizens have enough jobs. Their politicians aren't called racist for caring about their people. The Mexican government isn't considered racist for its immigration laws. Our nation was overwhelmed in a short period of time with millions of illegal immigrants from a third world country. Americans were called racist for saying it felt like an avalanche. I felt the same way. It was overwhelming to have to shut up and watch your community deteriorate because our politicians were encouraging illegal immigrants to come to America because they were able to get driver's licenses, welfare, jobs and buy cars and homes with loans from American banks.

Regardless of what country you're from or what your race is, if you are in the country illegally, you should be deported. I wasn't surprised when the Brexit vote won in England. I was in Europe recently and I saw the negative effects mass immigration have had there. Like in America, many European citizens are angry about wages being lowered as a result of immigrants, and some have lost their jobs to immigrants who work for less. The immigrants' lives are improving while poor European citizens are suffering. They too think their government doesn't have their best interests at heart.

Trump was onto something when he said nations should've gotten together to create a safe zone for people in the Middle East who are now refugees due to Islamic terrorists. Conditions that are prevalent in third world countries are spreading in Europe and in America and causing havoc for their citizens. I was surprised to see what has happened to Paris. I didn't feel safe there the way I did in the nineties. I felt uncomfortable riding the RER train that many of the immigrants' ride. There are many homeless people and some sleep on the street. I saw a Middle Eastern woman outside of a train station sitting down on the sidewalk. Her toddler child was naked and stooping to poop while people walked by. It's a shame what has happened to such a beautiful city. I also felt uncomfortable in England. It's also a very different place than it was in the nineties. People yell racism; however, the conditions aren't better as a result of immigration. Many Europeans feel uncomfortable in their own country. I didn't get the unique feeling of being in London because of the influx of Muslims. It seemed weird to see the streets dominated with women wearing long black dresses with burqas. Muslim men looked at American women dressed in our style of clothing like they wanted to attack them.

If our government wanted to have programs where people can come to America legally to work, the immigrants shouldn't be allowed to get welfare. Like Mexico's immigration laws, people who migrate to America should be self-sustaining. Not all illegal immigrants are honest, hardworking people. We have many who are only interested in committing crimes and taking advantage of our welfare system.

The purpose of the "Anchor Baby" protection in the 14th Amendment granted citizenship and equal rights to African Americans and slaves who had been emancipated after the American Civil War. The 14th Amendment states, "Every person born within the limits of the United States and subject to their jurisdiction, is by virtue of natural law and natural law a citizen of the United States. This will not, of course, include persons born in the United States who are foreigners, aliens who belong to the families of Ambassadors or foreign ministers accredited to the Government of the United States, but will include every other class of persons."

The 14th Amendment clearly states the "Anchor Baby" protection wasn't for foreigners. Illegal immigrants are foreigners in America. The 14th Amendment is being hijacked by our politicians to reward poor behavior by illegal immigrants by not deporting people who are in our country illegally. For years, politicians, mainly Democrats, have refused to vote in favor of not granting automatic legal citizenship to people who are born in the country illegally. Even though the 14th Amendment reads as it does, Americans are still called racists because they aren't happy about the negative effects of massive illegal immigration.

Chapter 11

The DNC: Featuring Frumpy and Frumpiest

There were things happening on the DNC (Democratic National Convention) stage that had me shaking my head in disbelief. Giving the stage to illegal immigrants to speak was shameful! Some spoke in Spanish and not English. One illegal immigrant woman who'd received a deportation letter was honored on stage with her eleven-year-old daughter who was born in America. By doing this, Hillary and the DNC were endorsing people who have entered America unlawfully and they also sent a shout out for more immigrants to come to our country illegally.

The eleven-year-old girl met Hillary at a rally where she expressed her worry about her mother being deported. Hillary reassured the young girl that she would do whatever she could to help her and her family. Another woman who is an illegal immigrant spoke Spanish when speaking on the DNC stage. She said our government needs to fix our immigration system in order for families to be able to live out the American Dream. The American Dream is supposed to be for people who are in our country legally. Our immigration policy is broken because our laws aren't enforced. I think this comment was disrespectful to American citizens and to immigrants who came to our country the legal way.

Hillary is a pimp; however, this was Big Momma pimping! How shameful! If I entered someone's country illegally, I would've at least made an effort to learn to speak that country's language, and I definitely wouldn't call a nation's citizens racists because they were upset about wages being lowered and the loss of jobs that were given to millions of illegal immigrants. If I had entered a country illegally, I would show my gratitude for getting welfare and birthing children who got automatic citizenship by at least learning the country's language, and I definitely wouldn't commit criminal acts. As an illegal immigrant, I would absolutely not burn a country's flag when the country I was in illegally treated me better than my native country.

The president of the United States' job is to implement and enforce laws written by our congress, not to encourage or aid and abet illegal immigrants. Hillary is more concerned with helping illegal immigrants live the American Dream more than she is in helping poor black Americans and poor Americans of all races gain the opportunity to live the American Dream.

I find it interesting that Black Lives Matter members don't seem to connect the dots with poor education, loss of jobs and more crime in their neighborhoods with our politicians cosigning on massive illegal immigration.

On the first night of the DNC, American flags weren't obviously visible. After Americans made a fuss about the lack of flags, Democrats made sure there were several American flags that were on the stage and in the hands of people in the audience. Some Americans think it's shameful or embarrassing to have American pride. One of the many beauties about President Ronald Reagan was his high pride for the United States of America, and he didn't minimize his proudness for this great nation.

I think Bill and Hillary Clinton are both smart politicians. I think they're both moderates. The true Bill and Hillary probably have more Republican political views. I think Hillary and Bill know what they should do as politicians; however, their need to win at whatever cost makes them panderers. Hillary and Slick Willie were confident that Hillary would've won the 2008 Democrat presidential nomination over Barack Obama because they think they're smarter than most and they've gotten away with a lot over the years. Divine intervention isn't only at play with Trump. Hillary is in the hot seat, too. It was divine intervention that caused her to lose the 2008 Democrat nomination. She probably hasn't recovered. Some think she stayed with Bill after the Monica Lewinsky scandal because of her need for power and to be president one day.

Trump and Hillary are people who are used to getting what they want and winning at whatever cost. The DNC and the RNC had uncertain and disharmonious energies because they were dealing with situations that they didn't know how to harness. Divine intervention is making Hillary's life difficult by having to run against a candidate like Trump. Though she publicly said she wanted to run against Trump, I think inside she was hoping he would be the last person she would have to run against because he's unpredictable.

I wasn't blown away by any of the speeches given at the DNC nor the RNC. I felt sad and emotional when I saw the parade of black mothers on the DNC stage who were wearing red corsages. Some seemed to have needed dental work and one looked like she needed teeth. I hope someone from the DNC has offered to buy dentures for her. These mothers' sons were killed by police officers. I felt they were pimped big time because people of all races have been killed by the police. However, white mothers, Asian mothers and Latino mothers weren't honored. According to Snopes.com, in 2015 there were 1,388 people who died at the hands of police, 560 were white and 318 were black, and 510 were from other races.

Though the majority killed weren't black people, some can argue that there are more black people killed by police because they are a smaller percentage of the population. Even with that argument, many would have a different perception of police only killing black people if the media reported the police killings of all races. The DNC was careful to not put mothers on the stage whose children were killed by illegal immigrants.

The media is guilty of not reporting the many police killings of non-black people. When media outlets report stories about white police killing black men, there are often protests, riots and looting in poor black communities. Other races don't burn down their communities and target police officers to kill when someone of their race is killed by a white police officer. The media likes the sensationalism ghetto blacks give when a black person is killed by a white police officer.

There were some family members of slain police officers who spoke at the DNC. Though they got a few minutes to speak, the black mothers wearing red corsages solidified the belief that their sons were killed because of white racist police officers. The women got a loud standing ovation. It wouldn't have mattered if any of their sons had a gun pointed at an officer's face when they were shot and killed.

Obama and Hillary are smart politicians. If they showed an array of mothers of various races who have had children killed by police, it would dilute the belief that it's open season on killing black men in America by white police officers. This was a disingenuous act with an energy of dishonesty. Some of the children of the mothers who wore red corsages on the DNC stage had questionable behavior with their interaction with the police when they were killed, but that doesn't matter. As long as America exists, the fact that black people were once slaves, the guilt of many will always give sympathy to the black person, regardless of their behavior.

There were too many speeches that tried to solidify Trump and the Republicans as racists. The more I heard these kinds of speeches, the more it made me wonder who are the real racists.

Michelle Obama's presentation at the DNC was a good delivery; however, I didn't believe her when she began to speak highly of Hillary Clinton. Actually, I didn't think any of her speech came from her heart. She said in her speech, "I wake up every morning in a house that was built by slaves, and I watch my daughters, two beautiful intelligent, black women, playing with their dogs on the White House lawn. And because of Hillary Clinton, my daughters, and all of our sons and daughters, now take for granted that a woman can be president of the United States. So, don't let anyone ever tell you that this country isn't great, that somehow, we need to make it great again, because this right now, is the greatest country on earth."

I was happy to hear Michelle Obama have gratitude for America, because I remember in 2008 when Obama was campaigning, she said, "For the first time in my adult life, I am really proud of my country because it feels like hope is finally making a comeback." Before her husband ran for the presidency, he attended Columbia and Harvard University and he was a senator. Michelle attended Princeton and Harvard University and she worked at a law firm. She wants to reprimand Trump for wanting to make America great again; however, some feel she and Barack benefited from affirmative action. Michelle didn't seem to think America was the greatest country on earth in 2008.

I am happy she seems to have found gratitude for the many opportunities this great nation offers. Some people were offended because in her speech Michelle said the White House was built by slaves. The White House was built by black slaves, free blacks and some white people. I didn't find her comment offensive; however, I do think it was another way to remind people that America had slaves and this is a racist country!

Michelle Obama has come a long way. In 2012 on "CBS This Morning" she said, "I'm not some angry black woman." This may be true; however, when Obama first hit the campaign trail there were times when Michelle did look angry. Maybe she wasn't angry, however I did see angry expressions on her face. Though she is a Harvard and Princeton graduate, I still felt her demeanor was often angry at times and I had a strong feeling she was a sister from the hood who could throw down if she had to. I don't think this is a negative. Being versatile can be an asset. Whoever helped her with her personality and her appearance make over did a fine job. Watching Michelle over the years reminded me of the old TV show, "Leave It to Beaver," because Michelle transformed into a chocolate June Cleaver.

I don't know where to begin with Bill Clinton's DNC speech. When he started speaking about the special woman he had eyes for while in college, I was wondering what woman he was speaking about. Usually, someone who is that much in awe and love with their mate doesn't become the type of womanizer that he was. Maybe Bill and Hillary had the kind of special love story he spoke about; however, I didn't believe him. Bill's story would've been more believable if he would've at least mentioned that he and Hillary had some challenges in their marriage.

As I've said, Bill Clinton and Ronald Reagan were my two favorite presidents. They represented a time in America when American pride was seen as something honorable. During Clinton's presidency in the '90s, the economy was good and race relations didn't seem to be as bad as they are now. I enjoyed America more during this time because the problems were mainly between black people and white people. I think immigration can be beneficial, however I don't think poor Americans have benefited from the massive way illegal immigration has swept into our country. During Clinton's presidency, Americans made decent salaries because the American worker was a commodity. Today, many of those workers have been replaced by illegal immigrants. Bill was a moderate and his welfare overhaul helped a lot of poor people make better choices. Some went back to school and some had fewer babies.

Bill Clinton is just a fraction of the man he once was, and I am not speaking about his age. That special spark he had is gone. He seems like a bitter, cranky old man. He's lost his magnetism. He and Hillary may be a power couple; however, if you feel you are forced to be in a relationship with someone you don't love for political power, it can kill your spirit. Maybe it wouldn't be as bad if Bill hadn't gotten caught with Monica Lewinsky years ago because he could've continued to have affairs (maybe he still have them). If I was a man, Hillary wouldn't be the kind of woman I would want to cuddle with.

Many say Trump is a narcissist. The definition of narcissism is: The pursuit of gratification from vanity or egotistic admiration of one's attributes. The term originated from Greek mythology where the young Narcissus fell in love with his own image reflected in a pool of water. Trump is a loud, bragging, shoot-from-the-hip type of a man who lets it be known that it's about him. A narcissist can also be a smooth, quiet type person who puts effort into making his or her deeds appear to be selfless when the foundation of their motivations are for their self-serving ego. Trump is clear about who he is.

All of our presidents are narcissists. I have always been suspecting of many of Obama's motivations. He seems overly concerned about manipulating his legacy the way a skilled chess player would make his moves.

TRUMP ... Divine Intervention or Not?

Obama is okay with negative feedback from Republicans, however he doesn't seem to want to rock the boat with groups like Black Lives Matter, Muslims and illegal immigrants. It's rare you'll hear him point out poor behavior from these types of groups.

President Barack Obama's speech at the DNC made him sound like a narcissist. I was distracted during his speech because I saw visions of neon pink and green elephants in my mind's eye on the stage because of what he was *not* saying. He mentioned himself 119 times. His speech seemed more like a ploy to convince the American people that he was a good president for years. He didn't get into how conditions are worse in the black community since he's been in office for over seven years. He didn't mention how wages were down for unskilled workers. He briefly mentioned ISIL, but he didn't say anything about radical Islamic terrorists. I think it's important for the president to state his accomplishments; however, his speech was more about what he did and less about what he thinks Hillary would do. If he would've elaborated on what Hillary could do better as a president, it would've put a damper on his mediocre presidency.

Obama didn't speak about securing our southern borders and he didn't speak about the poor conditions massive illegal immigration has caused in poor black communities. He didn't speak about the San Bernardino, California terrorist attack. He didn't mention solutions for the many homicides that happen in the south side of Chicago and other urban cities.

The president briefly mentioned our veterans and police officers. However, I didn't get the feeling that he had love for them. I felt he threw them into his speech out of obligation. This would've been a perfect time for him to chastise Black Lives Matter or any group for publicly chanting they want cops physically harmed. Obama's speech wasn't on the level of what I think a speech should've been from a president whose country is in trouble. I was able to decipher the truth from his speech based on what he did not say. Like his wife Michelle, I didn't believe Obama when he spoke highly of Hillary because the tension between them is thick, whether it's verbalized or not.

I have seen Chelsea Clinton give better speeches than the one she gave at the DNC. I understand she recently had a baby, however she seemed as if she had something personal going on. Someone made a joke on television, "Chelsea Clinton's speech was like a Chinese restaurant after midnight. They don't deliver." She seemed nervous and she didn't seem present. I've liked Chelsea over the years. I like the way she stays out of the limelight and she doesn't seek media attention. When Hillary walked out on stage after Chelsea's speech, it was endearing to see a mother and daughter embrace each other, however it did seem staged. It seemed like they were having a countdown of an exact amount of moments they would hug before Chelsea walked off the stage.

Hillary Clinton wore the best pantsuit I've seen her wear at the DNC for her speech. The Ralph Lauren white pantsuit was a good choice. Years ago, comedians made jokes about her ankles and called them "cankles," because they are thick. Hillary stopped wearing dresses that showed her legs. On occasion, she would wear maxi dresses however now she's resorted to wearing pantsuits. When I was growing up, I was teased because I was skinny and I had thin ankles. In the black community, you're picked on if you have skinny legs. It's common to see black women with thick legs and ankles who are proud to show them off. I hoped Hillary would dress how she wants to and not decide her fashion based on how others think. People picked on her ankles (cankles) and now they make fun of her pantsuits. If you're going to be made fun of, it's best to be picked on when you're at least doing things your way.

Hillary's DNC speech wasn't memorable. She tried hard to be human and personable. It's difficult for me to listen to her speak because she sounds robotic and insincere. I turned the television volume on low and I had to make an extra effort to stay focused on her lackluster speech. She got on the dump Trump train too. Trump was mentioned 451 times at the DNC. I often hear people say Trump doesn't have a plan. I didn't hear much of a plan from Hillary other than raising taxes and ensuring illegal immigrants they will get legal status.

Early into her speech Hillary said, "Now we are clear-eyed about what our country is up against. But we are not afraid. We will rise to the challenge just as we always have. We will not build a wall. Instead we will build an economy where everyone who wants a good-paying job can get one. And we'll build a path to citizenship for millions of immigrants who are already contributing to our economy." Notice she didn't say illegal immigrants. I don't think a presidential candidate should start her speech with pimping votes from Latinos by rewarding illegal immigrants for their poor behavior. Her opening speech should focus on American citizens and how she can make our lives better.

Some think Hillary is the first woman to run for president. These women also ran for president: 1872—Victoria Woodhull, Equal Rights Party; 1940—Gracie Allen, Surprise Party; 1972—Shirley Chisholm, Democrat; 1972—Linda Jenness; 1972—Patsy Takemoto Mink, Anti-Viet Nam War Candidate; 1988—Lenora Fulani, New Alliance Party. Did you also find it interesting that the so-called first woman to run for president (Hillary) didn't use her DNC speech as a platform to speak out against the violence, killing and abuse that's done to Muslim women in the Middle East? I was wondering if her silence was paid for by the millions she's gotten from Saudi

Arabia, Kuwait, Oman, Qatar, and other Middle Eastern nations for the Clinton Foundation.

The DNC members would like for you to believe it was a love fest at their 2016 convention. On the news, there were reports that noise machines were used to drown out the many boos Hillary got from Bernie Sanders supporters. When Bernie said, "We have to elect Hillary Clinton," the crowd booed. They also booed loud during Senator Cory Booker's speech when he mentioned Hillary.

Chapter 12

The RNC: Bombastic and the Silver Fox

The smartest thing Trump has done so far was selecting *Indiana Gov. Mike Pence as his vice-presidential running* mate. Pence has a cool demeanor; however, he also speaks with wisdom. At first, I was disappointed when Trump didn't choose Newt Gingrich as his VP. After seeing and listening to Pence, I thought Trump made an awesome choice.

Pence has the Bill Clinton effect on some black women. I think Pence is handsome and his demeanor gives him unique sex appeal. I was surprised to hear so many black women say the same thing. He is a calming effect to Trump's bombastic and sometimes fiery shoot-from-the-hip style.

I like Donald Trump. He's often misunderstood. Granted, sometimes he makes it easy for people to mangle what he says. My Jehovah's Witness mother doesn't believe in voting; however, she said she thinks Trump has a good heart. I agree with her. Trump probably cares more about ethnic people and all races of people more so than the politicians who call him a racist.

In 2012, when Obama was running against Mitt Romney for president, VP Joe Biden was speaking at a rally with several black people in the audience. Speaking about Romney, he said, "He's going to let the big banks once again write their own rules—unchain Wall Street!" He then added, "They're going to put y'all back in chains with their economic and regulatory policies." When I share this with black people, they are shocked. They hadn't heard about it because the media didn't splash the story because a Democrat was the offender. If a Republican said the same, it would've been considered racist and you would've heard from Jesse Jackson and Al Sharpton. Biden's comment made me wonder who wants who back in chains.

Hillary is notorious for speaking about Jim Crow. When the state of Alabama closed 31 driver's license offices, she accused Republicans of discrimination and trying to make it more difficult for black people to vote. Democrat representative Debbie Wasserman Shultz said Republicans were trying to resurrect Jim Crow laws in the form of stricter laws at the state level because they wanted voters to have a valid identification to vote. She said this law would restrict African Americans and Hispanics from voting. Jim Crow were state and local laws enforcing racial segregation in the Southern United States. These laws restricted civil rights, civil liberties and denied the right for blacks to vote.

As a black woman, I find it insulting that Democrats think that I would think the closing of DMVs and having to have an identification document to vote means Republicans want to send my people and me back to the Jim Crow era. Black people are resourceful, and we're capable of getting a ride wherever we want to go. I've heard some people say that poor people can't afford to get identification documents. The government provides housing, free medical care and food stamps for poor people, so getting these same people a $15 identification card shouldn't be a big deal. Instead of Democrats calling Republicans racist for wanting voters to have identification documentation, they should use their energy to make it more convenient for poor people to get identification documents and create more options for voting like increasing mail-in ballots.

I think it's foolish to let anyone vote without having identification. Voting is a right; however, the government should know who the individual is who is exercising their right to vote. The "chains" and the "Jim Crow" comments seem more racist than Republicans wanting people to have voter identification. If Trump used this same language you'd hear, "Racist, racism!"

The RNC (Republican National Convention) was clear that Republicans are proud of the American flag. There were several flags on the stage and audience members proudly waved theirs. I was happy to see this level of American pride. Our government has its issues, however I am so thankful for being in a country where I am able to have a platform to create change, because my predecessors, black people, white people and other races fought to make changes that allow me the many freedoms I have today.

The DNC and the RNC both had some spirited speakers. Hillary's name was only mentioned 247 times, half of the amount of times Trump was mentioned at the DNC. Tiffany Trump was one of my favorite speakers at the RNC. She started her speech by apologizing. She said, "Excuse me if I'm a little nervous. I never expected to be here tonight addressing the nation. I've given a few speeches in front of classrooms and students but never in an arena with more than 10 million people watching. Ha, Ha. But, like my father I never back down from a challenge." My Speaking 101 class taught me to not point out the negative to your audience. Listeners may not realize you're nervous until you point it out.

Maybe Tiffany made an apology because she wanted to minimize how professional she was as a speaker. Some people may have been turned off by her being such an outstanding speaker because of her young age. She was the most natural speaker at the RNC. She has a big, bright, colorful creative aura that's magnetic.

Though she made an apology about being nervous, her spirit was probably saying, "Damn, I am good. I got this!"

When Trump's wife Melania stepped on the stage wearing that fabulous white dress, I thought, "Wow! She's wearing the hell out of that dress and I want one." At the time, I thought the talk the next day about Melania would be how beautiful she looked in her Roksanda Margot balloon cuff dress. Instead, the talk was about the mishap in her speech.

Melania looked beautiful, but she did seem to struggle with delivering her speech. She's no Tiffany when it comes to speaking, however she seems like a smart woman. Yes, Melania is an attractive woman but I think if her hair flowed more and if it was a bit bouncier, it would give her a softer, more relaxed look. She's probably a warm woman, however her demeanor is stiff and her hair seems like it's over sprayed with holding spray. She was accused of plagiarizing Michelle Obama's 2008 speech. There were similar words and sentences in her speech that sounded like Michelle's 2008 DNC speech. Interesting, some had accused Michelle of plagiarizing Saul Alinsky in her speech. Saul was an American community organizer and writer. President Obama was accused of plagiarizing former Massachusetts Gov. Deval Patrick on a few occasions. In 2008, Hillary accused Obama of plagiarism for using Patrick's words. Obama told reporters he should've credited the former governor for using a passage he delivered.

President Obama nor Michelle's plagiarisms got the massive reporting in news outlets. I would love to help Melania craft a speech. I would have her write her own story from her heart. Then I would help her polish her words by editing her heartfelt words so they sounded like they came from her. I found it disappointing that Melania's speech writer wasn't a better coach to help her cultivate a speech from her own unique American story and her past from growing up in communist Yugoslavia.

Melania speaks five languages, Slovenian, Serbian, English, French and German. Some bash her for posing nude in the past for magazines. I'd probably pose nude too if I had a body like hers. She should be proud of her beautiful body. I think nudity is beautiful and we've all seen naked body parts. If Trump becomes president, Melania will be the hottest first lady we've had. There was a black female congresswoman, Joyce Beatty, who wore the same white balloon cuff dress at the DNC that Melania wore to speak at the RNC. There were internet polls with both women side by side; the question was: Who wore it better? My black friend said she voted for Melania and she got a backlash from some black people. I think both women looked nice in their dresses; however, I think Melania went beyond wearing the dress—she slayed it! My vote went to Melania, not because of her race, but because I felt she simply looked better in the dress. Because of Melania's speech, we were all given a divine intervention lesson: Be real, authentic and speak from your heart regardless of the backlash you may get.

The RNC theme was "Make America Safe Again." Rudy Giuliani is old school and he comes from a period where respect for authority was a given. I believed Rudy when he spoke about his appreciation for our men and women who are our police and military. He had a lot of passion when he spoke at the RNC. He tends to say things that some feel is controversial. However, I understand how he thinks because I am a former police officer and I got to see what happens on the streets of America. Though there are some bad seeds who are soldiers and police, I also understand that police and soldiers give a lot of themselves to protect our nation. This was one of my favorite parts of his speech: When police come to protect you, they don't ask what race you are. When they come to save your life, they don't ask if you are black or white, they just come to save you! I had that attitude as a police officer and it was rare that my fellow officers didn't think the same way.

Ivanka Trump's RNC speech was nice. She doesn't have the natural speaking flow of Tiffany; however, I think she delivered it the best she could. We aren't all good at everything. Ivanka seems to be a good business woman and mother. I felt she made an effort to loosen up.

Eric Trump did okay as a RNC speaker. He seems proud to speak about his father. There isn't resonance in his voice and sometimes his voice is high-pitched and this would make me not want to hear him speak for a lengthy period. Donald Trump Jr. got rave reviews for his RNC speech. I think he's a better speaker than Eric, however I think they both lack resonance in their voices. Their father has inflections in his voice and this makes listening to him more comfortable.

Trump and Ivana Trump, the mother of Ivanka, Donald Jr. and Eric, seem to be more youthful and energetic than their children. Ivanka, Donald Jr. and Eric seem proud of their father and they seem to look up to him. Sometimes the kids seem a bit stiff, as if they are trying to be perfect. All of Trump's children seem like exceptionally good children and their parents should be proud of them. Ivanka, Donald Jr., and Eric seem to have a high level of gratitude. Though they're rich, they seem to appreciate what they've learned and what they have.

Ted Cruz was a big highlight at the RNC. The first time I saw his face, I felt he was creepy and he didn't seem to be trustworthy. He was bold to show up to Trump's crowning as the Republican nominee for president and not endorse him. What Ted did to Trump would be the same as someone inviting cheerleaders to perform at their function in support of them and the cheerleaders show up and give the person who invited them to perform their middle fingers. In his speech, he said, "We deserve leaders who stand for principles, who unite us all behind shared values, who cast aside anger for love. If you love our country and love your children as much as I know you do, stand and speak and vote your conscience."

If Ted was willing to cast aside his anger for love, he would've been able to honor his pledge about supporting whoever won the Republican nomination. Ted made no mention of Trump. As he spoke, the audience shouted, "Endorse Trump" several times. He refused to mention Trump and the audience started to boo him. Trump made a visible entrance on the stage and clapped while the audience booed Ted. Ted then said, "I appreciate the enthusiasm from the New York delegation." Security rushed his wife Heidi out of the room. Ted finally took his pacifier out of his mouth and said he would vote for Trump.

Mike Pence looked sexy standing in front of a blue background that matched his blue tie at the RNC. The blue background complimented his white hair. He looked like a silver fox. His demeanor isn't too hot or cold. He has a perfect temperament for Trump. He knew when to give a dash of humor. There's a humility about Pence. I enjoyed his speech; however, I enjoyed looking at him more.

It was smart to give Pence a blue background to speak in front of and then bring Trump out with several flags behind him when he spoke. I felt emotional with the high energy in the room while people waved their flags. They weren't shouting USA and waving their flags because they'd been criticized for not honoring our flag. This audience was filled with people who are proud to be American citizens. Trump standing on that stage reminded me of President Ronald Reagan because his American pride was glowing. I enjoyed Trump's speech, however I think it was too long. One of my favorite things Trump said was, "The most basic duty of government is to defend the lives of its own citizens. Any government that fails to do so is a government unworthy to lead. It is finally time for a straight forward assessment of the state of our nation. I will present the facts plainly and honestly. We cannot afford to be so politically correct anymore."

I say, "Amen."

Trump's stance is much different than Hillary's and Obama's, who call Americans racist for not being happy about deterioration in our cities, loss of jobs, crowded schools and more crime as a result of illegal immigration. In 2009, while giving a speech in France, Obama said Americans are arrogant, dismissive and derisive. He was all of those descriptions because of what he said. The way Muslim men treat women in the Middle East is much harsher than Americans being arrogant, derisive and dismissive. It was rare that he said negative things about Muslims. Of course, there are some arrogant, dismissive and derisive Americans; however, he was in France where they are boldly arrogant and they will verbally tell you they don't like Americans. In the '90s, I was in France and we were told by some restaurant employees that they wouldn't serve us because we were American. Not serving us was quite arrogant, dismissive and derisive.

Because Obama was a member of Reverend Wright's church for many years, it makes me wonder if he truly has love for America. When he does attempt to speak highly about Americans and America, it seems forced and insincere. He called us these names while in a country where many hate America. It's rare I don't agree with Trump. Sometimes I disagree with the manner in which he expresses how he thinks. I'd rather have the bombastic Trump over pandering, pimping Hillary any day.

Chapter 13

God, Trump, Spirituality and Politics

The definition of politics is: Activities that relate to influencing the actions and politics of a government or getting and keeping power in a government. The opinions that someone has about what should be done by government. A person's thoughts and opinions about politics. Based on this definition, I don't understand why some people think politics, religion or spirituality don't merge with each other. Spirituality relates to our physical, spiritual, emotional, mental and spirit bodies, which are a part of politics and every human situation.

I am no longer a practicing Jehovah's Witness; however, I grew up as one. Jehovah's Witnesses don't vote because they say the Bible teaches that the highest allegiance of the faithful is to God himself, and Witnesses take that to mean they will not give allegiance to other entities, people, the American flag or authorities. They translate voting for a political figure as an act that goes against what their God wants for them. They think they must remain separate from societies in which they live in order to maintain their strength of faith and character. For these reasons, they don't vote, fight in wars or celebrate holidays.

Today, voting is an honor for me because I often remember the many sacrifices my black fore parents made for us to have the right to vote. I am not religious. I say I am spiritually connected to the universe because I think more of life happens in the invisible realm than it does in our physical reality. I don't know, nor can I prove, that a God or a supreme being that's greater than man is responsible for creating the universe, planets, galaxies and life. I am not afraid to use the word God, though I am more comfortable saying "universe" when speaking of mystical, spiritual or supernatural occurrences.

In 1870, the 15th Amendment gave black Americans the right to vote. Literacy tests and poll taxes were some of the obstacles blacks faced in the south and other states to forbid them their voting rights. Medgar Evers was a civil rights leader during the sixties. He and some other black ex-servicemen went to a Mississippi voting booth in 1963 to vote when they were stopped by a mob of white men who wouldn't allow them to vote. Evers said this about that incident, "All we wanted to do was be ordinary citizens. We fought during the war for America, Mississippi included. Now, after the Germans and Japanese hadn't killed us, it looked as though the white Mississippians would."

While carrying a stack of T-shirts that read, "Jim Crow must go," Evers was killed by a rifleman who shot him in the back. Evers was one of many black people and people of other races who were killed, beaten and threatened for their fight to give black people their 15th Amendment right. One of the reasons I share this story is because I do think God/Universe uses people to help enact the necessary changes we need in our world. Of course, Jehovah's Witnesses have the right to not vote; however, if Medgar Evers was a Jehovah's Witness, I doubt we would know about his heroic story.

Jehovah's Witnesses' reasons for not getting involved in politics make it sound as if God only uses humans who aren't his servants to be a part of necessary changes in our world that have to do with politics. Maybe Jehovah's Witnesses don't think it's their duty to put in the necessary energy to help to create a better world when it comes to politics. I think our world would be in more disharmony if all people had the beliefs of Jehovah's Witnesses.

Just think, we wouldn't have MADD (Mothers Against Drunk Drivers) if Candy Lightner, the founder of MADD, had not started her organization after her 13-year-old daughter was killed by a drunken hit and run driver. Lightner was instrumental in politics because her organization helped the need for legislation that gives stricter penalties for driving while intoxicated. I've yet to attend a church where the politics of the church weren't in play. Jehovah's Witnesses have drama and politics happening in their congregations too. Politics run rampant in churches and every area of our lives. Because you don't actually "vote" doesn't mean you aren't part of politics that happen in every area of life.

There are some things that aren't explainable. Change is inevitable, yet we don't always have change play out the way we think it should. Some think change should be easy and it shouldn't create havoc, anger and anxiety. I've accepted that I don't always get what I want, however I do get what I need. I think God has his/her spotlight on Trump. With the magnitude of Trump's ego, I don't think there is anything that would've given him the life lessons he's faced since entering the presidential race.

God? Again, I don't know if there's a supreme being that presides over all life and the universe. I am a mystical, spiritual person because I grasp life more when I connect the physical part of life with the invisible realm. I hear more in what's not being said. I see more than what my physical eyes see. I hear more than what my physical ears hear. Maybe what I described is God. For the purpose of this book, I will say the word God when speaking of divinity and the supernatural.

A quote from my Ce Ce "Confucius" Ferrari collection of quotes says, "A man stood up and shouted, 'I am the smartest person in the room.' He then looked around to realize he was the only one in the room." I think Trump is learning that he doesn't have all the best answers for all situations. No one human has all the answers. As much as I think I know, I also realize I don't know much. When I think my mind is made up about something or someone, I still like to hear feedback and suggestions from others. This attitude has made a major shift to help me have a happier, more harmonious life. There was a time I had a need to be right and it was difficult for me to admit to myself or others that I was wrong about something. I think wisdom allows you to recognize your choice or decision may not be the wisest all the time.

Trump is in the hot seat. His soul and spirit are getting lessons that he probably thought were meant for other people. Trump is getting several opportunities to show that he doesn't have the power to maneuver every aspect of the election the way he can or has with his businesses. The presidential election is a whole new kind of an animal for him. The lessons his ego and spirit are getting are being observed by the world. At some point, every human will experience sitting in the hot seat. Race, financial status, education, nor your sex determines who gets in the hot seat. Every human experience this heat at some point in life. It can come through the form of illness, death, suicide, divorce, break-ups, financial loss, career loss, loss of cars and homes and other material possessions.

No human escapes God's hot seat, because this seat is necessary for every human's growth and transformation. Divinity is part of every human's life. What "happens" to us are opportunities for us to rise, evolve and transform. During a broadcast on Fox News,

Trump told host Megyn Kelly, "If I don't go all the way and if I don't win, I will consider it to be a total and complete waste of time, energy and money."

When I heard his comment I said, "Ouch!" He's not getting it. Trump has already created great change. Say what you want about this man; however, he had a great feat in knocking down 17 career politicians with the assistance of social media and not having to spend what traditional politicians spend for election campaigns. Trump has given more encouragement to people who aren't rich to use social media to gain political office. He's allowing us opportunities to grow and improve ourselves as we observe outcomes and reactions of his unconventional behavior. Trump is teaching us lessons of how to be and how not to be. He is a giant mirror of our own inner ego. We all need to see our own inner Trump.

Because of Trump, more Americans are publicly speaking about their dissatisfaction about illegal immigration. I think the Trump factor helped Bernie Sanders get a larger following. After Hillary called Trump a sexist several times publicly, Bernie seemed to have gained more supporters after Trump brought up Bill Clinton's sexual assault allegations from the past. For me, Trump winning isn't the most important factor in the 2016 presidential election. I am excited about the changes that are coming and have already happened as a result of Trump. Hopefully, Bernie made a deal with the Democrats to make changes with their super delegate voting system. Trump has been clear that he's a winner. I've learned that sometimes in life when you think you're winning, you're losing, and sometimes when it may appear you're losing, you're actually wining. I had to change my definition of what winning is for me.

If I based my need to win solely on what our culture has said it should be, I would expend a lot of energy in what can often be empty victories because a lot of energy would go into trying to play into some else's idea of what winning is. Sure, I understand there are some standard ways of winning in our world, however I think it's also important to know when your supposed win is not truly a gain. When you tap into God/Universe, mysticism and spirituality you're able to see more than just the determinations of our culture and world. The greatest gift of growth and transformation could be in what is perceived as a loss. This is why the invisible, spiritual part of life is important to connect with because you're able to gain higher understandings about yourself, others and situations. I think Trump is gaining some great lessons about losing and winning when you put spirituality into the mix.

Melania Trump shouldn't be underestimated because she's attractive and she was a model. I like Melania. I think she would make a lovely first lady. I like the way she doesn't seem needy for media attention. She seems comfortable in her skin and staying in her lane. Regardless of their beauty or age, it's rare I meet women who have her level of inner comfort. If The Donald was to leave her today, I have a feeling she'd be just fine. Of course, she'd do well financially, however I also think mentally and emotionally she'd be healthy. When I tap into her spirit and aura, I get the feeling of a woman who has grown a lot during her time with her husband.

During a Morning Joe segment, Melania was asked about her feelings on the language her husband uses. She said, "Well, do I agree all the time with him? No, I don't and I tell him that. I tell him my opinions; I tell him what I think. Sometimes he listens, sometimes he doesn't." Maybe Trump will learn to listen more to the counsel of his lovely, regal wife. I have a strong feeling that she gives him wise advice. The Donald has been chosen to gain lessons in grace and humility on the world's stage.

No other human has battled modern day political correctness like The Donald. He reignited our right to use the First Amendment.

Chapter 14

Does Carly Have a President's Face?

I like a lot of things about Trump, however he's made some blunders along the way. During the 2016 presidential campaign he gave some politicians names that stuck to them like an eel sucking your blood. Trump called 5-foot, 8-inch-tall Marco Rubio, Little Marco. Little Marco finally got fed up and called Trump out for having small hands. Trump then said Little Marco had big ears. I hadn't noticed the size of Trump's hands or the size of the Little Marco's ears until they picked on each other.

Marco Rubio was speaking about Trump at a rally when he said, "You know what they say about men with little hands." The audience laughed. "You can't trust 'em."

That comment didn't sit well with Trump, so he defended his manhood during a presidential debate. Referring to Rubio, he said, "He hit my hands. Nobody has ever hit my hands; I've never heard of this before. Look at those hands, are they small hands? And he referred to my hands; if they're small, something else must be small. I guarantee you, there's no problem. I guarantee it."

I was watching the debate and I hit the rewind button a few times on my DVR and laughed several times. This was the first time I heard a man defend the size of his "Johnson" during a presidential debate. Black men call their penises "Johnsons." No way would a black man let you get away with calling their penis small! I wondered if Trump's need to defend the size of his

"Johnson" meant he had some brother in him. After the debate, Trump continued to publicly defend the size of his hands. I wondered how Melania felt and what she thought about her husband defending the size of his package publicly.

Trump refused to participate at the GOP debate that was held before the Iowa Caucus because he felt Fox News host Megyn Kelly was rude to him because of the first question she asked him at an earlier GOP debate. "Mr. Trump, one of the things people love about you is you speak your mind and you don't use a politician's filter. However, that is not without its downsides, in particular, when it comes to women. You've called women you don't like fat pigs, dogs, slobs and disgusting animals."

"Only Rosie O'Donnell," Trump fired back.

Megyn Kelly is good at what she does as a Fox News commentator and I enjoyed watching her show. I do think it was strategically set up for the female on the debate panel to ask Trump this kind of question. By having a female ask Trump this question, it made him look more distasteful to many women. I can understand why Trump was pissed, however I don't think he should've made it out to be such a major deal. Because Megyn Kelly was going to be on the debate panel for the GOP debate before the Iowa Caucus, he refused to be a part of the debate. I was disappointed that he refused because most of the polls showed him winning the caucus. I thought if he didn't show up it could hurt him. His absence from the debate allowed people to take a closer look at Cruz. Maybe some people thought it was petty for Trump to skip the debate because of Megyn Kelly.

Trump lost the Iowa Caucus by a few numbers. I felt he would've won had he participated. This was another powerful lesson for The Donald. This is an example of the ego appearing to win temporarily but in the long run, you are actually losing. Maybe Trump losing the Iowa Caucus has helped him internally. I've learned to put my ego aside and wave the white flag and surrender before I lose more. Years ago, a therapist said to me, "It's like you're in a large coliseum ready to go into battle with your sword. There aren't any spectators in the coliseum and you don't have an opponent. You're having a battle within yourself and you need to decide when you're going to stop fighting with yourself." Because of the way Trump handles some situations, sometimes I see a vision of him holding a sword and having a solo fight in an empty coliseum.

Some may think I defend Trump when his behavior is poor. I will call anyone out when I think they have behaved poorly, my relatives and myself included. Because I am able to decode what Trump says, I don't automatically think what he says is racist.

"Look at that face, would anyone vote for that? Can you imagine that, the face of our next president?" This was a comment Trump made about Carly Fiorina to a *Rolling Stone* reporter. This comment and the one about Rosie O'Donnell are equally distasteful. At first, Carly wouldn't entertain Trump's comment publicly. I was happy she made that decision because I didn't want a lot of talk being made about her face because that would make people focus on her face even more. At a GOP debate, Carly made a comment in reference to Trump, "I think women all over this country heard very clearly what Mr. Trump said."

"I think she's got a beautiful face and I think she's a beautiful woman," Trump said. When I heard that I said to my television, "Liar, liar pants on fire." Carly does have an interesting-looking face; however, I don't think she's ugly. Trump speaks how he thinks and he often says what many are thinking. Some think only women who run for office are criticized for their looks. Secretary of State John Kerry and former Congressman Newt Gingrich don't necessarily have attractive faces. Some people felt they didn't have a president's face either.

Chapter 15

Hillary, Trump and the KKK

August 31, 2016 was Donald J. Trump Day! It started with him going to Mexico and meeting with their president Enrique Pena Nieto. He looked like an American president and he handled himself with grace and professionalism while on the stage in Mexico. In the past, Trump has said that Mexico will pay for the wall to be built. Some criticized him for not having a discussion about who was going to pay for the wall to protect American citizens on the southern border. Trump said he didn't discuss who would pay for the wall with the Mexican president; however, Enrique Pena Nieto said he told Trump Mexico will not pay for the wall. It was difficult for some in the media to give Trump a compliment for his meeting with the Mexican president, so they harped on the idea that Trump didn't tell the truth about discussing who would pay for the wall to be built. Nieto seemed to be impressed with Trump.

If president, Trump would institute a program that would require all foreign money transfers and wiring from financial institutions and companies like Western Union to have to verify legal United States status. Mexicans who work in America send an average of 24 billion dollars a year to Mexico. Most of the workers are illegal immigrants. The Mexican government would have to make a onetime payment to the United States government of 5 to 10 billion dollars to ensure 24 billion can continue to flow into Mexico. An increase in visa fees and trade tariffs can be added and enforcement of existing trade rules would generate revenue. Money that's given to Mexico for aid can be deducted from the monies the United States government has to pay for welfare for illegal immigrants from Mexico. The United States has the right to cancel our visa program because immigration is a privilege—not a right. The way some illegal immigrants behave, you'd think it was a right for illegal immigrants to come to America. America has taken in four times more immigrants than any other country, and this has caused low-wage jobs and higher unemployment for legal citizens.

After Trump's visit to Mexico he went to Phoenix, Arizona to give a speech about his 10-point immigration plan. He was on fire! It was refreshing to hear someone speak publicly who cared about the welfare of Americans first and not be embarrassed to say that the needs of Americans come first. Some people complained that Trump doesn't have a plan. Well, he knocked it out of the park that night with his immigration speech. On day one of taking office, he would start the process of deporting two million illegal immigrant criminals.

1. Build the wall
2. End catch and release
3. Create a deportation task force and focus on criminals in the country illegally
4. Defund sanctuary cities
5. Cancel Obama's executive actions that will award amnesty to millions
6. Extreme vetting—block immigration from some nations
7. Force other countries to take back those who the U.S. wants to deport
8. Get biometric visa tracking system fully in place

9. Strengthen E-verify, block jobs for the undocumented
10. Limit legal immigration, lower it to "historic norms," and set new caps.

There were some people, mainly Democrats, who were offended by Trump's immigration speech. He didn't say anything racist and it made it difficult for his opponents to complain. They said they didn't like his tone. He did a great job and he only spoke the truth. It's about time we have politicians who think and speak highly of Americans and put our welfare and safety first. People enter our country illegally and have anchor babies who have legal citizenship, and now Trump is the bad guy for breaking up families. Illegal immigrants can take their children with them back to their countries. The anchor baby rule needs to be revamped to end this abuse.

KKK (Ku Klux Klan) member David Duke going public with his endorsement of Trump put The Donald in an exceptionally bright spotlight because his adversaries used it against him. Instead of right out denouncing David Duke, Trump danced around and said he didn't know David Duke. I don't think Trump is a racist. I think he didn't boldly right away denounce Duke because he wanted to get votes from racists and non-racists so he could win the election. David Duke launched a Senate race in Louisiana because he said he was inspired by the nomination of Trump. Trump eventually made a publicly clear denunciation of Duke on NBC'S "Meet the Press" to host Chuck Todd.

Democrats loudly accused Trump of being a racist and implied he had ties to the KKK. Millions of Americans aren't aware of the original Democratic Party. The KKK was founded in Tennessee immediately after the Civil War. The group was formed for former Confederate soldiers whose influences spread through the decimated United States. Their principle was: Launch a reign of terror against Republican leaders black and white. After Abraham Lincoln was assassinated, the Klan's anti-Republican ideology spread rapidly.

In 1868, the Klan's activities sped up and they caused more brutality. The election that pitted Republican Ulysses S. Grant against Democrat Horatio Seymour was crucial. Republicans continued programs that prevented southern whites from gaining political control in their states. Klan members knew that given the chance, blacks would've voted Republican. Across the south, the Klan and other terrorist groups used brutal violence to intimidate Republican voters. In Kansas, over 2,000 murders were committed in connection with the election. In Georgia, the amount of murders was higher. 1,000 were killed as the election neared. In these states, Democrats won decisive victories at the polls.

The message I get from modern-day Democrats isn't about a movement to truly help poor people. The Democratic Party would be the number one party to fight against illegal immigration if they first cared about poor Americans because the piling of millions of poor illegal immigrants into America hurts poor Americans. The back in the day Democrats realized the way to get black people and poor white people to vote for them would be to give them "free" stuff. Democrats aren't interested in explaining the breakdown to poor people that everything has a cost and the tax payers would have to foot the bill for their so-called "free" stuff. The "free" stuff and the enforcement of black people being victims keep poor people tied to the umbilical cord of mommy and daddy government.

Instead of Democrats killing thousands of people so that there would be less Republicans to vote, their new strategy is to get America to be browner and have open borders to allow as many poor people into our nation with the hopes they will vote Democrat. By doing this, Democrats can count on more Electoral College votes from districts that are heavily saturated with poor, ethnic brown people because Electoral College votes are determined by legal and illegal residents. Should the millions of brown people who have entered the country illegally one day get amnesty and be awarded citizenship and get the right to vote, the Democrats would pray that these new multi-millions of citizens would vote Democrat for the rest of their living days.

I think the commercial in support of Hillary showing KKK members wearing their costumes and hoods saying they support Trump as a way to connect Trump to the KKK went too far. I would feel the same way if a commercial was made about Hillary's connection to Seddique Mateen, the father of Omar Mateen, the shooter at Pulse nightclub in Orlando that killed 49 people. He said his son shouldn't have attacked the club because homosexuals will be punished by God. Where is the liberal outcry over such a comment? It would've been a lashing for days in the media if a Christian or a Republican said the same after lives were taken in a terrorist attack. It's interesting how Muslims and Christians have the same biblical belief about homosexuality, birth control and abortions, however, Democrats and liberals seem more understanding of Muslims not accepting homosexuality. What's up with that?

Mateen was shown in the audience at a Hillary rally in Kissimmee, Florida which isn't far from the location of the shooting. Mateen ran for president of Afghanistan, supports the Taliban, Hamas—a militant fundamentalist organization who wants to destroy Israel, and Hezbollah—an Islamist militant group in Lebanon.

Hillary hasn't repudiated Seddique Mateen, yet pressure from Democrats was put on Trump to denounce the KKK. If a commercial from Trump supporters showing Hillary and Mateen at her rally showed a video of airplanes going through towers at the World Trade Center, suggesting that Hillary is a terrorist, there would be anger from the left. I hope no one makes such a video. KKK Grand Dragon Will Quigg said he was retracting his endorsement of Trump and he would endorse Hillary.

Hillary didn't denounced Mateen or Quigg. Divine intervention is at play here and we're all being asked to have integrity. Hillary's afraid to denounce Mateen because she needs Obama's campaign support and she doesn't want to offend Muslims. Where is the outcry from the same people who bashed Trump because of his KKK endorsement? Why not do the same for Hillary? Will the group who made the video about Trump and the KKK now make a video commercial linking Hillary to the KKK because a Klansman has endorsed her? This is a perfect example of hypocrisy, and all Americans are full of the big "H."

In 2010, Hillary commemorated late Senator Robert Byrd by saying: "Today our country has lost a true American original, my friend and mentor. It's almost impossible to imagine the United States Senate without Robert Byrd. From my first day in the Senate, I sought out his guidance and he was always generous with his time and wisdom." Maybe this is one of the reasons Hillary so easily throws around "Jim Crow" at her rallies. Byrd was a KKK member who led his local Klan chapter. Many years later, Byrd did make an apology. If Trump said the same, Democrats would use this against him, even if the former KKK person made an apology.

Hillary does talk down to people. I think Hillary and Democrats talk down to black people because they pimp us by keeping the rhetoric about Republicans stopping black people from being successful when they know in 2016 any race person can be successful if they're willing to educate themselves and do the necessary work, and have habits that support their success. I think Hillary and Democrats talk down to black people when they pretend black on black crime isn't an issue, yet they use every opportunity to showcase black victims who have been killed by white police officers as they ignore black-on-black crime. When Hillary comfortably speaks at rallies to black people and tells them the Republicans are sending them back to the Jim Crow era, and when Joe Biden says, "They're going to have y'all back in chains," when speaking to a black audience, I think black people are being talked down to.

The movie "Straight Outta Compton" was based on the life of the rap group NWA. I enjoyed the movie and I learned more about the life of the group's members. In the movie, it showed the high tensions with the police and the black community. I've always had a difficult time understanding how some black people criticize the white man and the police for mistreating them and for killing black people, yet we harm ourselves more than any other group in America. Black people should be the group that treats each other the best because of slavery, racism and the many injustices we've endured. Watching "Straight Outta Compton" was painful because I saw my people get mistreated by their own race and the police.

Chapter 16

Angry Gold Star

Trump often brags about his billions of dollars and says he's funding his own campaign. When I received letters and emails asking me to donate to his campaign, it was difficult for me to readily write a check because I felt as rich as he is, he didn't need my money. I eventually made a donation because I wanted to support him, because I do like his tone about bringing law and order back to the White House.

Sen. John McCain was a former Navy pilot who spent over five years in a notorious North Vietnamese prison called "Hanoi Hilton." He was beaten repeatedly and tortured and spent two years in solitary confinement. He's not a fan of The Donald. "Trump is dangerous because he fires up the crazies within the Republican Party," McCain said.

Trump responded, "He's not a war hero because he was captured. I like people that weren't captured, okay? I hate to tell you. I believe that perhaps he's a war hero but right now he's said some very bad things about a lot of people."

Trump got a backlash from some veterans because of his comment. I think what McCain and Trump said was offensive. Trump supporters didn't appreciate being called "crazies." McCain speaks harshly of Trump; however, his comments were immature and unprofessional for a senator to make. I think McCain dissed American citizens just because they support Trump.

Gold Star father Khizr Khan, a Muslim American, spoke at the 2016 DNC with his wife by his side. A Gold Star person is an immediate relative of someone who was killed while serving in the military. I felt he and his wife's love for their son who was killed while serving in Iraq in 2004. Humayun Khan took 10 steps forward to check out a suspicious vehicle. The car bomb exploded. He saved the lives of the soldiers he supervised. I am thankful and grateful for Humayun Khan for serving in our military and for protecting the rights and freedoms for our country.

Mr. Khan was angry with Trump for wanting to ban Muslims from coming to the United States. He pulled out a pocket-sized copy of the Constitution from his suit jacket and held it in the air. "Donald Trump, you're asking Americans to trust you with their future. Let me ask you, have you ever read the United States Constitution? I will gladly lend you my copy. In this document, look for the words, liberty and equal protection under the law!"

He was referring to Trump defending the right to waterboard our enemies while at war with the hope of getting necessary information for the safety of our soldiers and country. I wonder if Khan gave Hillary a pass for not responding to Christopher Stevens' 600 requests to get more security in Benghazi. Stevens and three of his men lost their lives when the compound was attacked. Maybe he also gives her passes on having a private server for her classified emails and for erasing over 30,000 emails and for not being truthful about the content in the emails, and aiding and abetting illegal immigrants.

Khan is probably quite aware of Hillary's pay for access with the Clinton Foundation. According to Breitbart.com, Khan is a lawyer who helps rich Muslims buy their way into America through our EB5 government program, which is a national security risk. Foreign operatives can use the program to gain entry to the United States. If this is true, a Trump presidency which would be cautious about people migrating to America from terrorist-laden countries could put a damper on Khan receiving large amounts of money for bringing in rich Muslims to the United States. Websites Therealside.com and Govtslaves.info reported that Khan was given $375,000 from the Clinton Foundation after speaking at the DNC.

In Khan's DNC speech when speaking about Trump, he also said, "You have sacrificed nothing and no one."

Trump's response was, "I think I've made a lot of sacrifices. I work very, very hard. I've created thousands and thousands of jobs, built great structures. I've had tremendous success. I think I've done a lot."

I think Trump had a misstep in how he responded to Khan when he said, "If you look at his wife she was standing there, and she had nothing to say. Probably, maybe she wasn't allowed to have anything to say, you tell me, but plenty of people have written that. She was extremely quiet and it looked like she had nothing to say." Trump actually said what I was thinking, however, I think he should've responded by saying, "I would like to invite Mr. Khan to sit with me and have a conversation."

Pat Smith is a Gold Star Mother. Her son was killed in the Benghazi terrorist attack and in her speech at the RNC, she blamed Hillary Clinton for her son's death. She said, "Donald Trump is everything Hillary Clinton is not. He is blunt, direct and strong. He speaks his mind and his heart and when it comes to the threat posed by radical Islamic terrorism, he will not hesitate to kill the terrorists who threaten American lives. He will make America stronger not weaker. This entire campaign comes down to a single question. If Hillary Clinton can't give us the truth, why should we give her the presidency?"

Some in the liberal media went wild. Smith didn't get the same warm, soft, treatment of, "You can say whatever you want to say because you're a Gold Star Parent." Trump was vilified by Democrats and Republicans because of the way he responded to Khan's speech. MSNBC'S Steve Benen said Khan's speech was memorable and Pat Smith's speech was offensive. The Washington Times had an article entitled, "Respect for A Mother's Love Is Rationed" in response to the vilification of Smith's speech. The title says a lot. MSNBC'S Chris Matthews said, "I don't care what that woman up there, the mother has felt. Her emotions are her own. But for the country in choosing a leader, it's wrong to have someone get up there and tell a lie about Hillary Clinton. It's not true. It's logically not true. I think it's wrong that they ruined their evening with this."

Josh Rogin from the Washington Post said, "I feel for Pat Smith but the RNC and Trump are using her and her son's death for politics and that's wrong."

After Khan's DNC speech, Josh Rogin said, "Khan's speech was a nod to those people who have been bothered or demonized by Trump." Interesting, he didn't seem to think Hillary and the DNC were using Khan for political reasons just as the Republicans and the RNC used Smith.

It is hypocritical to demean a Gold Star Parent's message because they don't support the candidate of your choice while you praise another Gold Star Parent's speech whose words were equally as harsh. I don't think a Gold Star Parent or anyone should have automatic immunity from people criticizing them when they publicly criticize others. Just because you have a dead child who gave their life for our country shouldn't be a reason for a Gold Star

Parent to be disrespectful to those they disagree with, and they shouldn't think they're immune from criticism.

Because Trump hasn't lost a child doesn't mean he hasn't experienced loss. I think Khan was wrong to say Trump hasn't sacrificed anything. Every human has losses, and because Trump doesn't publicly tell us what his losses have been, either emotional or physical doesn't mean he hasn't had losses. I've met people who put down people who are emotionally attached to their animals and who are sometimes more emotionally traumatized than people who have lost their human loved ones. Emotions are emotions regardless of what they're attached to. You may think a human life is superior to anything else on the planet, but that doesn't mean that there are people who have equal and maybe a higher intensity of emotions that are attached to other forms of life and maybe things. I had a friend who reprimanded a coworker because she was crying for days over her dog who died. The owner of the dead dog was offended and purchased a book for her coworker to read so he could learn to have a deeper understanding of human emotions for animals.

Trump has a dead brother, mother and father. Because some say the greatest loss is that of a child, doesn't mean that others who don't have dead children feel less pain. There are some spiritual practices that believe that extended mourning isn't healthy and whether you are mourning the loss of a child, animal or anything else it's not beneficial to your mind, body and spirit to not heal from your loss and pain and move forward and live in the present. Because you mourn your child or anyone doesn't automatically mean you love them.

Khan was popular for a minute, however as reports went public about his connection to the Clinton Foundation and his law firm practices of bringing over wealthy Muslims, he disappeared from the media. Is Khan a (con) Khan?

Chapter 17

Here Comes the Judge

Observing the 2016 presidential race was like watching a game of ping-pong. One day there was something in the media that smeared the Trump campaign and the next day Hillary's campaign got trashed. I see it as divine intervention balancing out our crap. Dr. John Demartini is a provocative inspirational speaker. He believes everything has value regardless of how bad or awful we think something may be. Demartini said magazines that trash celebrities are good because they help celebrities keep their egos in check. Celebrities are put on high pedestals, and the gossip magazines diminish them often with truths that they wouldn't want the public to know about. I see this dynamic happening with Trump, Hillary and all Americans. Everybody's stuff is flipping out into the spotlight. The Karma Gods are on patrol 24/7.

Years ago, there was a lot of talk about how the world would come to an end in 2012. Many astrologers said the Age of Aquarius started in 2012 as we ended the phase of the Piscean age. The Piscean age was about, "Oh Lord save me." The Aquarian age is about, "I am the Power, My God is within me, and Save thy self." This doesn't mean that I don't believe that there isn't a God force in the universe but rather the God force is saying to us to use our inner God power and resources that we have. Jesus represents the Piscean age where we were victims and needed a power outside us to take care of us.

The Aquarian age is more like Jesus saying, "You can do this. I've already demonstrated to you what is possible." The Aquarian age is asking us to be our true, authentic selves. We are being asked to awaken the God within us rather than rely on the God we've been conditioned to believe that resides outside us.

Based on some astrologers, 2012 was an ending and death in a spiritual and a symbolic way. It was an ending to a world that we once knew and an end to our old selves. This is one of the reasons I think we have such an unconventional candidate like Trump running for president. In my personal life, I notice that the Karma Gods show up faster than ever. When I am being the best I can be and I am living and speaking from integrity, the Karma Gods reward me with gifts and blessings. When I am not being the best I can be, I have problems and disharmony in my life. This doesn't only apply to me. This applies to all humans, rich, poor, male, female, and all races. No one is exempt. We may try to run, but we can't hide. Some way, somehow, we all get caught and have to sit in the hot seat.

When Trump first announced he would be running for president, I thought he should've immediately reached out to the black community. I don't mean just connect with some famous black people who are celebrities, leaders and pastors. He should've made contact with the black community by having speeches and rallies in black neighborhoods early on. He should've gone into black communities and had town hall meetings with everyday folks and listen and speak to them about their fears and concerns. It would've been a good idea if Trump would've made connections with some business people who would've been willing to bring decent-paying jobs into black communities and have them speak at his rallies. Some black people are interested when you use black people who are Republicans to speak to them. A white Democrat is more acceptable to some black people, more so than a black Republican is. Omarosa, Ben Carson and other black Republicans aren't going to have the same effect as Trump himself would've had by speaking personally to the black community. I think many in the black community would've appreciated Trump embracing them right away because the black community has been let down by Democrats and Republicans for decades.

Trump finally made an invitation to the black community and he visited a black church, The Great Faith International Ministries in Detroit, and gave a Unity speech. Some felt his appearance was a little too late. There were some angry protesters and there were also some protesters who were angry because they couldn't get a seat inside. I understand how a lot of the poor people felt. Poor people think the same way when it comes to getting tickets to presidential debates. It seems like the rich politicians and rich people give their seats to their friends.

Trump would've been smart to get a campaign movement set up in the black community shortly after he announced he was running. The campaign team should've been made up of mainly people from the black community. This would've made many in the black community feel like they were a part of his movement and not feel they were just being pimped at the last minute. If he had campaign members from the black communities, the residents would've trusted Trump and his message more.

Mark Burns, a black pastor, gave a high-spirited speech at the RNC. At a rally, he said, "Bernie Sanders doesn't believe in God. Bernie gotta get saved. He gotta meet Jesus. He gotta have a 'coming to Jesus' meeting." Bernie Sanders says he's not an Atheist, he's Jewish. Burns was bashed recently for retweeting a picture of Hillary Clinton in black face. He made an apology. Burns has been called out for making false statements on his website. He first said his website had been obviously hacked or someone added the information. He walked out of a CNN interview because he didn't like the questions he was being asked about his resume. Burns made this apology: As a young man starting my church in Greenville, South Carolina, I overstated several details of my biography because I was worried I wouldn't be taken seriously as a new pastor. This was wrong. I wasn't truthful then and I have to take full responsibility for my actions.

On his website, Burns said he'd earned a Bachelor of Science Degree and spent six years serving in the Army Reserve. He wasn't ever in the Army Reserve; he was in the South Carolina National Guard and was discharged in 2008. North Greenville University told CNN he only attended the school for one semester. Burns admitted he didn't finish his degree. Trump's team should've vetted him before aligning with him and having him speak at the RNC. Because he wears the title of pastor doesn't mean he has integrity. This is a beautiful story of divine intervention putting the spotlight on Burns' lack of authenticity. His belief in God doesn't seem to have helped him with his honesty, and this makes him a hypocrite. Many call Hillary a liar, however we are all liars. A lie is a lie; however, the worst kind of liars are those who hide behind God and religion. If Burns believed what he says his God is capable of doing and being, he wouldn't have had the need to lie about his credentials on his website because God's love and power isn't off limits to people who don't have college degrees.

Some people said CNN was wrong to call him out. I think CNN did the proper thing and it doesn't matter what race or political affiliation someone is. Wrong is wrong. He lied!

Trump's bluntness often gets him into trouble. Trump University was being sued because the plaintiffs said they were duped into paying tens of thousands of dollars on the belief they would be trained to learn Trump's real estate strategies. I understood what Trump meant when he said this about Judge Gonzalo Curiel, a Mexican American, who is presiding over the lawsuit in a Wall Street Journal interview. "United States District Judge Gonzalo Curiel had an absolute conflict in presiding over the litigation given that he was of Mexican heritage and a member of a Latino Lawyers Association."

Judge Curiel is a member of the La Raza Lawyers of San Diego, who work to create a path to immigration reform, a path to citizenship and reduced deportations. Trump thinks the judge should recuse himself because there's an inherent conflict of interest in the Trump University lawsuit. Trump said, "If he was giving me a fair ruling I wouldn't say that. I'm building a wall. I'm trying to keep businesses from going to Mexico."

Most people in Trump's position would probably think the same way; however, Trump spoke out loud what most of us would keep to ourselves or would only share with family and friends—not in the media. I think Trump was harshly ridiculed on this one because the story about the judge's affiliation with La Raza wasn't being told as often as Trump's comments were being repeated. The fact that Trump thinks the judge wouldn't give him a fair hearing because he's a Mexican alone is racist. However, when it's combined with his La Raza association and who and what Trump stands for, I think it's understandable for Trump to think the way he does about this matter. Trump would've done better to say, "Because of the judge's association with La Raza, I don't think I would get a fair hearing because I am not in favor of amnesty."

Chapter 18

Mirror Mirror on the Wall—Who Has the Most Beautiful Daughter of All???

One of the most outstanding things I think about Donald Jr., Ivanka and Eric is their high level of gratitude and appreciation. I think Trump and Ivana did a good job in instilling and teaching their children the importance of values. Trump is surrounded by beautiful women in his family. At the Indiana primary coverage, MSNBC host Chris Matthews was heard off mic commenting on Melania Trump. "Did you see her walk? Runway walk. My God is that good." Matthews doesn't think much of Trump, however it's nice that he admires something about Melania.

Donald Jr., Ivanka and Eric have similar auras. It's almost like I am reading the same person when I tap into each of their auras. I am able to do this through my psychic abilities. Yes, I am psychic and so are you! We were born with psychic abilities. Our psychic abilities are like exercising our muscles; they get stronger the more we exercise them. I don't mean they have similar auras because they're siblings and they were raised by the same parents. This is something different. It's like they are the same person. I have three siblings, and we have three obviously different auras though there are some small similarities.

Donald Jr., Ivanka and Eric did a campaign advertisement called Millennials for Trump. The ad read: This is not a Republican vs. Democrat election. This is about an insider vs. an outsider. People on Twitter and Instagram went wild making fun of them. Granted, the picture looks kind of strange and I agree with some critics who say they look emotionless. They may have physically been together when they took the picture, however the photo looks poorly Photoshopped, with Eric's photo looking like it was thrown in at the last minute. Some said they looked like the actors from the "Children of The Corn" movie, the Menendez brothers and horror movie actors. Is there such a thing as being too likeable? I think people on social media had a field day with this ad because the Trump kids seem to do everything perfectly and some were happy to be able to dump on them.

It is interesting how The Donald is always wearing a suit and tie, even when he goes to baseball games. Tiffany seems to have a more fluid, artsy aura. Every family has a star; I don't mean a Hollywood star. I am speaking of the family member who is the most unique, has the largest aura and an off color one. The Donald is the star of his family. Barron is unique and he's the star out of the five Trump children. When Trump is long gone, the world will be graced with his "mini me," Barron. He's an interesting soul. He is more like Trump than his older sons are. If I had an opportunity to have a conversation with any of the Trump children, I would want to speak with Barron.

All of the Trumps seem like good people. I like Melania's energy a lot and I think she has a good core. She's my favorite Trump! I don't think she's malicious. Most people nowadays have corrupt cores even if they pretend they're good. What I said about the older Trump children isn't about condemning them. Whenever I see them, I see neon pink and yellow elephants in my mind's eye and that tells me there's more going on than what my physical eyes are seeing. Because I am a Trump supporter doesn't mean that I will pretend I don't see things that aren't perfect about him and his family. All humans have issues. I think Trump will evolve and transform greatly when he's able to distinguish the difference between someone being critical of him out of sheer hate, or when someone is giving him constructive criticism because they care about him and they want him to succeed. When I listened to the harshest criticisms about myself I was able to make major changes.

Trump has made some questionable comments, however at the same time he makes me ponder if we humans really want people to "just be honest and always tell the truth." Trump doesn't have a filter, and though he verbally speaks what many are thinking, he makes some people feel uncomfortable with some of his remarks. Years ago, on "The View," Trump and Ivanka were guests. He was asked how he felt about Ivanka posing nude. "I don't think Ivanka would do that (pose nude for photographs) inside the magazine. Although she does have a very nice figure. I've said that if Ivanka weren't my daughter, perhaps I would be dating her. Is that terrible?"

Joy Behar responded, "Who are you? Woody Allen?"

In 1994 a New York Daily News reporter interviewed Trump. He said, "I love creating stars and to a certain extent I've done that with Ivana. To a certain extent I've done that with Marla and I like that. Unfortunately, after they're a star, the fun is over. It's like a creation process; it's almost like creating a building. It's pretty sad."

When Ivanka was 22 years old, Trump was on the Howard Stern show. "You know who's one of the great beauties of the world according to everybody? And I helped create her. Ivanka. My daughter, Ivanka. She's six feet tall; she's got the best body."

In 1994 Trump was on the show "Lifestyles of The Rich and Famous." Robin Leach asked, "What does

Tiffany have of yours and what does she have of Marla?"

"Well, I think she's got a lot of Marla. She's a really beautiful baby and she's got Marla's legs. We don't know whether she's got this part yet (gestures towards his chest) but time will tell."

The list of bizarre comments Trump has made goes on and on. I don't think his compliments about his daughters' physical beauty mean he would like to commit incest with them. I met a woman years ago who was a stripper. Her parents and siblings would go to the strip club to watch her dance. They were proud of her and thought she was an artistic dancer. Many fathers probably think the way he does; however, they wouldn't dare verbalize it.

Trump's an equal opportunity offender. He offends men and women. These are some of the things he's said: MSNBC'S Willie Geist is uncomfortable-looking. MSNBC'S Mark Halperin has sleepy eyes and doesn't have a natural instinct for politics. Commentator Bill Kristol is a dummy and he's dopey. "Meet the Press" moderator Chuck Todd has sleepy eyes. Columnist George Will is broken down, boring and totally biased. I share these comments because some people think he only makes negative comments about women.

Trump has a point when he says people often make fun of his hair, yet he's called out for making comments about other people's appearance. Some may say you can change your hair; however, it's possible that people can be just as offended by people making jokes about their hair just as someone would be offended by someone calling them fat or ugly. He said, "Bette Midler talks about my hair but I'm not allowed to talk about her ugly face and body—so I won't. Is this a double standard?" I am not defending his behavior because it's immature, however, people who claim Trump has poor behavior are often a poor example of how he should behave. Hillary and other politicians condemn Trump for his immature behavior, however they behave poorly, too.

Chris Matthews said, "Hillary looked like Nurse Ratched, the antagonist in (movie) "One Flew Over The Cuckoo's Nest." He also said Hillary's appearance is witchy. Female hosts on "The View" ridiculed Trump for his negative comments about women and his remarks about Carly Fiorina's face, however former host Michelle Collins poked fun at her face too. Mimicking Fiorina, Collins said, "You know people tell me I didn't smile enough during the last debate." Collins imitated Fiorina's smile and then said, "She looked demented."

Joy Behar said, "I wish it was a Halloween mask, I'd love that." The women can hide behind saying they were only joking, however, if they were really into the sisterhood they would understand that Fiorina had already been beaten up in the media with Trump's comments. If Fiorina was a black female Democrat, I doubt the women would've made those comments. If there were Halloween masks of Fiorina's face and Behar's, it would be a tossup as to which face would be more popular for Oct. 31. If you had to choose, would you rather have Fiorina's face or Behar's face?

Chapter 19

Liar, Liar Pantsuit on Fire!

Hillary was looking pretty tired and worn. Earlier in her campaign she said she would love to run against Trump. She and her camp underestimated The Donald. I knew he would be a hell of an opponent. Lately, Trump had been looking tired, too. Both Hillary and Trump seemed to have gained weight. Maybe their stress level was high due to their campaigning and maybe they weren't sleeping and eating properly. I can relate because I've been having the same issues. I am doing a cleansing program, eating healthier and exercising regularly to get back on track.

Earlier in Trump's campaign, he had a rally in Las Vegas. I hopped on a plane to attend the rally because I find him entertaining and I love his blunt truth. This was before his rallies got violent and protesters lined the streets. We had to stand for hours because there were over 5,000 attendees and there were more who wanted to get in so they removed the chairs. Trump was delightfully entertaining. He said, "I just don't get Hillary. The first thing she does is get up in the morning and put on her pantsuit." He became funnier because he wasn't trying to be funny. There were people of all ages and races at the rally and it was peaceful and I felt safe.

Trump has a way of stepping into fresh poop and that gives his adversaries ammo to use against him. I knew he would be around for a long time because of the energy in the room. The crowd was in awe of him, not because he was a celebrity but because it was refreshing to hear someone who wants to be a politician speak highly of America and its citizens. I was jealous; I would love to boldly speak my unfiltered truths on a stage. Because of the politically correct police, many, especially white people, were afraid to speak out against illegal immigration because they didn't want to be called racists. Because of his bluntness and boldness to speak how he thinks, he's given many Americans the comfort of speaking how they think even if others disagree with them.

Maybe Trump was joking around and not really meaning for protesters or police to hurt people, however, it was poor behavior on his part to encourage rally attendees to be violent. When a black protester was apprehended by the police it was called racism. The media rarely showed white people getting kicked out of Trump rallies; however, they enjoyed showing black people being kicked out. There was a black man at a Trump rally who was accused of shouting at an elderly white man and shooting him the bird (with his fingers). The elderly white man punched the black man and the story got spun that Trump and his supporters are racists. If the white man shouted and shot the black man "the finger" and got punched, it wouldn't be called racism. This story sounds more like poor behavior colliding more than racism to me.

When Trump would make abrasive comments at his rallies it was difficult to defend him. At a rally he said, "If you see someone throw a tomato, knock the crap out of them, knock the hell out of 'em, would like to punch him in the face." I believe in peaceful protests and if I did attend someone's function as a protester, I would protest in a respectable way because I wouldn't want someone to ruin my function.

Trump's behavior at some of his rallies solidified he was a racist to many. Many people think the definition of Republican is "racist." Trump got tagged as a racist for posting a photo sitting at a desk with a taco bowl in front of him. The Facebook post said: "#CincoDeMayo the best taco bowls are made in Trump Tower Grill. I love Hispanics." People on social media went wild with racist quotes and memes.

I found it interesting that the media didn't hop on the racial comments made by DNC members in emails that were exposed by WikiLeaks. A DNC member poked fun at the name of an African American executive. Her name is Laqueenia. The DNC member said, "Laqueenia is a name! I'm sorry boo. I hope you got a raise with that title. Just kill me now." Another DNC email said, "DNC outreach to Latino voters—Taco Bowl Engagement." Another DNC email said they wanted to use Bernie Sanders' Jewish religion to weaken him in the eyes of southern voters.

The majority of Democrats and liberals aren't aware of this story. I posted this info on Facebook asking where was the outcry from my African and Latino brothers and sisters who like to call Trump and the Republicans racists. Can you imagine Trump doing the same? He'd be forced to wear shirts with a big "R" in the front.

Hillary did a press conference with the National Association of Black Journalists. There were some Latino reporters who didn't seem happy with her because millions of illegal immigrants don't have legal status. They came short of demanding amnesty now. Hillary said, "I will need people across our country to make it clear to their elected representatives that they are going to be held accountable for how they are going to act on immigration reform. I've already talked to some of my former colleagues in the senate. This will be fast tracked." Millions of Americans have made it clear to their elected officials how they feel about illegal immigration, and this is one of the reasons she's running against Trump. The Latino reporters had the power. Hillary looked pitiful and small at the press conference because at no time did she point out to the Latino reporters that the illegal immigrants broke our immigration laws and her number one priority is the American people. It's shameful that the people with the bad behavior are controlling the actions of our politicians.

In 1995, during his State of The Union Address, Bill Clinton got a standing ovation for his stance on illegal immigration. He said Americans were disturbed by the number of illegal immigrants in the country. He noted the burdens they put on the taxpayer. He added, "That's why our administration has moved aggressively to secure our borders more by hiring record numbers of new border guards, by deporting twice as many criminal aliens as ever before, by cracking down on illegal hiring by barring welfare benefits to illegal immigrants." This speech sounded like Trump's. President Clinton had a way of publicly speaking that made Americans feel like they were valued. Obama often reminds us that we don't measure up. A president would be called a racist if he delivered Clinton's speech today.

All politicians are pimps; however, the worst kind are those who use racism in their pimping scheme. When Flint, Michigan had its water contaminated with lead, Hillary publicly said the water problem lingered because of racism. This charge flew like a Boeing 747. Michigan's governor, Rick Snyder, is a Republican, so it didn't take much for Democrats and some black people to jump on board the racism plane.

In Hoosick, New York, state and local officials continued to tell the residents that their water supply was safe while knowing for a year it was chemically contaminated. Gov. Andrew Cuomo is a Democrat and the residents of Hoosick are mostly white. Cuomo wasn't called a racist for allowing his white constituents to knowingly drink contaminated water. This was hypocritical of Hillary and the Democrats to only use race in one scenario. Often, it's poor management and lack of integrity, not race, that causes politicians to falter in their jobs.

Politicians should be careful about throwing around the word racism because it doesn't help victims take personal responsibility for their lives. If victims constantly hear that their problems are based on racism, it prohibits them from making better choices in their personal lives because they think they're already doomed because of their race. If the city of Hoosick was a neighborhood with a majority of black residents, it would've been all over the news that white politicians ignored the water problem because they're racists.

TRUMP ... Divine Intervention or Not?

Chapter 20

Poor Bernie

I am still wondering what kind of a deal Hillary and Obama made with Bernie Sanders to keep him from publicly dissing Hillary. Maybe they agreed that if Hillary won she wouldn't run for president again and they would support him for the 2020 presidential election. Bernie got kicked to the curb in royal fashion. He didn't think Democratic National Committee Chairperson Debbie Wasserman Shultz had any intention of helping him win the Democrat 2016 presidential nomination because she's a Hillary supporter. Maybe Hillary and Obama promised Bernie they would revise the super delegate process. Super delegates are party members who are former presidents and major elected officials and they can switch their candidate support at any time. Hillary had more super delegates than Bernie.

Bernie wouldn't be my choice for president because he promises too much free stuff that isn't free because of the cost to American taxpayers. Kelly Mullen, a young woman activist, was a guest on Fox's Neil Cavuto show. Mullen organized a free college tuition movement. Over 100 colleges had students walk out of class in one day in support of Mullen's movement. She wants free college tuition at public universities, cancellation of all student debt and a $15 per hour minimum wage for all campus workers. Cavuto asked her who would pay for the free college. Her response was, "I'm not sure if you're talking about on a national level or at particular schools but I can sort of touch on that."

"Well you want all that free stuff. Someone has to pick up the tab. Who would that be?" Cavuto asked.

"The one percent of people in society that are hoarding the wealth and really sort of causing the catastrophe students are facing. I mean we have a relationship right now where the one percent of the population has more wealth than the 99% combined."

"Do you think the one percent could pay for all of this?'

"Absolutely, 85 people in the world hold more wealth than half of the global population," Mullen said.

Bernie Sanders tweeted support for Mullen's cause. I am for affordable college tuition; however, I don't understand why someone should get their tuition paid 100% by tax payers. We appreciate what we get more when we help pay for our choices. When I was a child, my doctor who was wealthy made his teenage children get summer jobs while they were in high school. They also had part-time jobs when they were in college. He helped them pay for some of their tuition; however, he believed that they would have more gratitude for their education if they helped to pay for it.

Many Americans complain about America being a capitalistic society. Capitalism has become a dirty word. A news street reporter was at a college asking graduates what they majored in. The reporter asked a young woman wearing her cap and gown what she majored in. "I have a business degree," she said.

"What do you think about capitalism?

"What's capitalism?" the graduate asked.

It's interesting when I hear rich celebrities voicing their complaints about capitalism because they don't get rid of their wealth that they think isn't fair and give it all to poor people. If everyone in my family was given a million dollars, the relatives who are responsible with their money would make smart choices and make their money grow and the irresponsible ones who are victims would be broke in a short period of time. My relatives and friends who do well financially have healthy habits, and my relatives and friends who are always struggling financially have poor habits. The majority of poor people wouldn't want the responsibility many of the one percent rich people have. There are probably millions of poor people who wouldn't want to do the necessary work to gain the wealth some of the 1% have because some of them worked hard for their money.

Bernie Sanders wanting to give free stuff to Americans wouldn't ensure there was equal effort. I used to do the hard work and put in the necessary effort to achieve extra money. I would then share my monies with irresponsible relatives and friends. No longer do I reward people who aren't willing to earn what they are given. I've given up a lot of my poor habits in order to find time to write and speak publicly. I had to learn to find solutions instead of making excuses. Television host Dr. Phil said, "If you want to find out why someone is slender, follow them around for a week and if you want to find out why someone is overweight, follow them around for a week. Different habits for different folks' equal different results. Many people today want the benefits without doing the work."

When Hillary called Trump a sexist, he took to the airwaves and brought up former President Bill Clinton's sex scandals. Trump said, "Hillary's married to the worst abuser of women in the history of politics." Bernie's poll numbers started rising after images about Bill Clinton and his sexual assault allegations and affairs resurfaced in the media. It was the Trump effect that gave Bernie a bump.

Bernie said that the collapse of Wall Street affected the black community more than any other community.

However, he never said that massive illegal immigration caused havoc in the black community because he too was pimping for the Latino vote.

I agree college tuition is out of control, however too many parents today don't want to accept who their children really are. Some people are suited for mainly retail-type work. By no means am I putting down retail employment. I personally know people who are in major debt because they felt their child who is basically a retail job person had to go to an expensive university. Daily people complain about 20-something-year old college grads who can't find employment in the area they have their degrees, yet more of the same caliber of students' parents still feel the need to send their children to expensive colleges and universities. I have a friend who is a flight attendant for a major airline. Her son wanted to work in the medical profession. She said, "I told my son I am not going to fly 150 hours a month so I can put him through college. I paid for him to go to a medical trade school and if he wants to go on to medical school he can pay his own way." She then said, "I have a life, too."

I have some flight attendant friends who are exhausted flying 150 hours or more monthly to put their children through college. They are always tired and depressed. They complain about having to fly so many hours. Many of them who have made this sacrifice tell me that their twenty-something and thirty-something-year-old children who have degrees are living at home with them and they aren't working because they can't find jobs in their chosen fields. A lot of parents try to keep up with the Joneses. With the number of young people who can't find jobs in their chosen fields, you'd think parents would work with their children to do more research on the kinds of jobs that would be lucrative before they get into debt with college tuition.

Some parents who have children, who are basically fit for retail work, want bragging rights. A young person going to college is one of those things that some think is "the thing to do" just as getting married and having children are. These kinds of parents want to brag about what university their child is attending or has attended. I know someone whose teenage child was struggling at a fancy expensive university. The teenager had some emotional issues. She would cut herself and she was suicidal. She often told her parents and grandparents that the university was too much for her and she didn't want to attend the school, but they insisted. The young woman wanted to work with animals and do artistic work, but that was embarrassing for her family and they insisted she remain at the fancy university. Her mother said, "Education is the most important thing." I agree with that, however, the best education for this young woman would be to learn about emotional/psychological health and to get some help. If you're an emotional mess and you can't function properly, your fancy degree won't help you. The family was more concerned about bragging rights than they were about the emotional health and welfare of their young relative.

Many people are becoming wealthy by creating businesses on the internet. More students should invest in trade schools. Years ago, more companies offered management positions and promotions from within their companies. Many positions were on-the-job training and didn't require a college degree. I am in support of our government encouraging and giving incentives to companies that give promotions to employees from within their companies. There are college coaches who help students choose career choices that blend with their passion and can be financially lucrative, too. Parents should do more research and help their children choose the best college career path instead of saying, "Just get a degree." I know someone who went to law school, and at 32 years old, he's living with his parents and he hates being an attorney. His student loan debt right now is $250,000. He, too, wanted to have a career doing something artistically, however that wasn't good enough for his parents. He's in the process of quitting law and moving to Hollywood to pursue something artistic in the film industry.

College is necessary for some professions; however, for some careers, people should find more inexpensive ways to learn their craft. Instead of taxpayers paying for free college tuition, I think our politicians should be in the business of coming up with more ways for people to gain education that's not expensive. They should encourage and support more vocational schools for junior high and high school students so they may go directly into the workplace after graduation should they decide not to attend college. There should be more government support and encouragement for students to attend trade schools. I think Bernie Sanders and any politician who are into giving "free" stuff to able-bodied people clip their wings and prohibit them from being the best they can be.

Chapter 21

"Basket of Deplorables"

The politically correct police defend minorities if they aren't Republican. If you're a black Republican or white Republican, you can kiss your politically correct protection goodbye! Hillary is supposed to be the unifier. Her slogan is: Stronger Together. With a slogan like that, I wouldn't expect her to call half of Trump's supporters a basket of deplorables. This is divisive language, yet she bashes Trump for being a divider.

Hillary doesn't call Islamic terrorists who killed Americans in San Bernardino and in Orlando at the Pulse bar deplorable. She doesn't call illegal immigrants who kill Americans deplorable, however, if you support Trump, whether you're a law-abiding citizen or not, you're still deplorable. Hillary thinks she can get away with saying such because she knows the politically correct don't support white Republicans. A Huffington post article entitled "Data Reveals Hillary Clinton was right about Donald Trump's Deplorable Supporters" says 40% of Trump supporters think blacks are more violent, more criminal, ruder and more lazy than white people. The data revealed 65% think Obama is a secret Muslim and 59% think he was born outside the United States. Regardless of the data, this doesn't prove the people in this survey are racist because of their answers. The question wasn't, "Are you a racist?" By the way, many black people agreed with these poll numbers because of their experiences, not because they're racist. Democrats who were surveyed showed their numbers weren't much different than the Republicans.

Black people are the race that's shown on the six-o-clock news for killing each other at a rate that's higher than any other race. White people and all race people are witness to the black on black murders and other crimes in Chicago and other inner cities. Of course, white people will think black people are more violent when they riot and then loot in their own neighborhoods as they claim they are angry with the white man for injustices. Based on the images white people see on the news, it's understandable why they think black people are lazier than white people. Before calling people racist, it's a good idea to understand why people think this way about black people. Every black person I personally know (including myself) has said something racist.

I don't know if Obama is a Muslim, however he sure does seem to go out of his way to protect them. Boy, does he get upset when Republicans say, "radical Islamic terrorists." I can understand why there was a mix-up about where he was born because there's literature from the nineties that says he was born in Kenya and raised in Hawaii. There's a promotional booklet from 1991 from his literary agent, Acton and Dystel, that says he was born in Kenya (Snopes.com). This may or may not be a mistake, however, when people hear and see conflicting info, they sometimes don't know what to believe.

A few days after Hillary made her deplorable comment, she nearly fainted and fell after leaving a 9/11 celebration in New York. Folks, there were definitely something going on with this election that's beyond the physical. This race was sporadic and unpredictable. News reports said Hillary had pneumonia. Whatever her illness was, I think the stress of her email saga, the public finding out about her aide hammering her 13 Blackberry devices, bleaching her server, the fear of which of her emails WikiLeaks Julian Assange may release, and the backlash from her deplorable comment put a health strain on her.

Divine intervention was kicking Hillary's ass! For a while it seemed like Trump wasn't going to stop his downward spiral, however, he revamped and his poll numbers started to rise even in swing states. Trump was doing well with the Karma Gods because it seemed he was listening to wise people. He changed his tone and stopped publicly defending negative things people said about him. I knew he would be rewarded if he did this. The Karma Gods were on Hillary's ass because she's fake. She won't be blessed or victorious for pretending to be a unifier, and she bashed Trump for being divisive when she did the same. Regardless of what Trump has said, her deplorable comment was toxic and I think it affected her health.

Feisty pollster Kellyanne Conway became Trump's new campaign manager and they seemed to be a good fit. Kellyanne seems to know what she's talking about. No one knew how long Trump would remain cool, calm and collected.

Chapter 22

Hillary: Your Husband is Bill "Deplorable" Clinton

The following is a blog I posted on social media in reference to Hillary's "basket of deplorables" comment.

Hi Hillary. I'm Ce Ce. I'm black and I am one of those 50% Trump supporters you called deplorable (irredeemable, disgraceful, shameful, dishonorable, unworthy, inexcusable, unpardonable, unforgivable, despicable) because I don't agree with illegal immigration. I am not a racist. I think one of the beauties in America is that we invite people from all over the world to be a part of our country legally. I am against illegal immigration because I've personally witnessed the damage illegal immigration has caused the black community. There's more crime, less jobs, wage decreases, crowded hospitals, housing costs have increased because of supply and demand, inner city schools are more crowded, which adds to the illiteracy rate of poor black children and all poor American children.

It's deplorable that you aid and abet illegal immigrants. Illegal immigrants spoke at the 2016 DNC (Democratic National Convention). You are a pimp. All politicians are pimps; however, you're the biggest one. You are pimping for the Latino vote. In a sense, illegal immigrants' votes do count because our elections are determined by the Electoral College vote—not a popular vote. Illegal immigrants are counted because electoral votes are based on the number of people that are in districts which are based on the census. It doesn't matter whether the people are legal or illegal citizens. With millions of illegal immigrants piled into poor communities, your chances of winning Electoral College votes are greater because they live in poor communities where people think Republicans don't care about them, and Democrats are their saviors so many poor people tend to vote Democrat. If you cared about poor people you should be the politician who is against illegal immigration because it harms poor black people and all races of poor Americans.

It's deplorable that you had black mothers wearing red corsages speak at the DNC who had children killed by police without showing mothers of all races who had children killed by police. Why did you ignore the pain of white mothers, Asian mothers, Latino mothers and other race mothers whose children were killed by police? You are a divider and you're causing more harm to poor black communities by perpetuating the myth that police are only killing black people, mainly black men. How disingenuous of you!

It's deplorable that while you were Secretary of State you weren't aware of Chris Stevens' 600 requests asking for more security at the Benghazi embassy. Your negligence attributed to the death of Chris Stevens and three other Americans who were killed in Benghazi during a terrorist attack.

It was deplorable for the nation who had to hear about your husband's DNA stain being found on Monica Lewinsky's blue dress. Some parents felt it was deplorable that they had to explain the definition of oral sex to their six-year-old children because of your husband's behavior in the Oval Office. Some find it deplorable that your husband was accused of several sexual harassment claims while president. Your daughter called Trump a "sexist." Does she also think her father is sexist?

It is deplorable that your staff Bleach-Bit your server to permanently erase your emails after you were subpoenaed. It is beyond deplorable that you had your staff break and hammer Blackberry devices with the hopes the trail of your emails would be gone forever. Hillary, you make mobster John Gotti seem like the J.V. (junior varsity) of mobsters. Hillary, you are gangsta!

It is deplorable that you criticized Trump for not immediately denouncing KKK (Ku Klux Klan) member David Duke. On Twitter you posted: On most campaigns there isn't much ambiguity as to who the candidate does or doesn't back. However, KKK Grand Dragon Will Quigg said he endorses you and he's donated thousands of dollars to your campaign. Did you publicly denounce him as a result and give him his money back?

It is deplorable that you've taken hundreds of millions of dollars from Saudi Arabia, Kuwait, Qatar, and other countries which persecute and kill women and gay people while you publicly say you're the champion for women and gay people.

It is deplorable that you call Trump and his supporters racist when you didn't publicly also call your unveiled WikiLeaks emails from the Democrat National Committee racist. These emails stated that the DNC campaign to get Latino's votes were called, "Taco Bowl Engagement." An email made fun of "Laqueenia," the name of a black businesswoman. Another leaked email showed an interest in using Bernie Sanders' Jewish religion against him in the South. This is the kind of behavior you accuse and chastise Trump and Republicans for. Where is the racism outcry from you?

It is deplorable that you claim to be the champion for women, yet as an attorney you represented a 41-year-old man who was accused of raping a 12-year-old girl.

There was evidence of the rape and you chuckled when your client passed a lie detector test. (Audio of Hillary on this matter is at: http://freebeacon.com/politics/the-hillary-tapes/)

It is deplorable that your husband played a modern day "emotional/mind" slave master when he recently publicly insinuated Trump's slogan Make America Great Again is racist. He said, "That message where I'll give you America great again is, if you're a white southerner—you know exactly what it means, don't you? What it means is, I'll give you an economy you had 50 years ago and I'll move you back up on the social totem pole and other people down." Granted, your husband publicly used this slogan several times in 1992 when he was campaigning. Apparently, your husband doesn't think much of black people either by using this tactic. Bill said this because of his fear of more black people awakening to you as a wolf in sheep clothing. It is evil to use slavery and the Jim Crow movement to scare an already depressed, poor community of people that their fate is dependent on making Hillary, who is the biggest pimp, hypocrite and race baiter, president.

Hillary, I was poor because I made poor choices. No white man, nor any other kind of man, or woman have ever stopped me from becoming or being anything, I choose. I am a proud black American woman and I think I have more opportunities because I am a black woman. You don't enforce the greatness that my people are capable of. Instead, you play into and perpetrate their smallness. This is eviler than anything I've heard Trump say or do. A great leader teaches people what they are capable of doing and being as a result of changing their poor habits to productive habits.

Of course, there are some Trump supporters who are racist, sexist, Islamophobic, homophobic, and xenophobic. You must also accept that you have supporters who are the same.

I am a Trumpette; however, I call Trump out when his behavior is poor, too. What you've said and done is worse than what Trump has said and done because you're pretending to be a woman who you are not. You are a divider. You and your boss, Barack Hussein Obama, seem to enjoy publicly dissing Americans; however, you make an effort to not offend Muslims and illegal immigrants. You are scarier than Trump because he's more authentic than you are. I pray Donald J. Trump wins the 2016 presidential election.

TRUMP ... Divine Intervention or Not?

Chapter 23

The Donald and the POPE

"**A** person who thinks only about building walls wherever they may be and not building bridges is not Christian. This is not the gospel," Pope Francis said.

Trump responded, "If, and when, the Vatican is attacked by ISIS, which everyone knows is ISIS'S ultimate trophy, I can promise you that the Pope would have only wished and prayed that Donald Trump would have been president." Eventually, Trump softened his stance with the Pope. Trump has a way of stepping into fresh poop; however, I felt Trump got a raw deal with the Pope controversy. I felt the Pope was out of line to say it's not Christian to build a wall. It's not Christian to not first take care of your immediate responsibilities and for a politician, that means the citizens they represent—not illegal immigrants. Because of massive illegal immigration, Americans are suffering. The Pope has elite armed warriors who protect him. Some Christians can judge him and say, "It's not Christian like to have guns on your premises." I think the Pope has the right to protect his property and Americans should have the right to do the same in the manner they see fit.

The Pope didn't mention the impact open borders have on poor American citizens. I am for change; however, massive immigration isn't change for the better. I think it's Christian to put the needs of your own people first. The Pope's comment about Trump referring to him not being Christian is judgmental. The Pope would be the first to say it's not Christian to be judgmental. I wonder if Pope Francis thinks it's Christian to invite millions of people to come and live in Italy without the approval of the Italian government because he wants to be nice to poor people. The Pope and Gold Star Parents are open to ridicule too if they condemn others.

The Pope often speaks about helping the poor. I haven't heard him ask, "How can the poor help themselves?" When you're poor and you make poor decisions that cause you to become poorer, you shouldn't expect taxpayers and others to support you financially. One way to ensure a life of poverty is to have children you can't afford. The fantasy that having children makes you happy is a myth. Having children or not having children doesn't ensure happiness. How you choose to live your life, with or without children, dictates your happiness. If you have children and you're stressed out all the time, you're not living a joyous life but rather a miserable life.

We are in the 21st century. Gone are the days when having several children was an asset so they can help you on the farm. Poor people having several children today are a burden on taxpayers and others. Being a burden to others doesn't seem Christian to me. I know a poor man who is on welfare. He has eight children and he brags that he's doing God's work by procreating. Parents who already have children who are on welfare and are receiving free lunch at school continue to procreate because other people step in and support the life choices they can't afford.

In 1996, President Bill Clinton reformed the welfare program and women were no longer rewarded extra money based on the number of children they had. The number of children black women had decreased. I was happy to see this, because the majority of them were struggling financially before they had one child. Latino women, mainly illegal immigrants, are having more children than other women of race in America. Something needs to give with modern-day religious rules about birth control. I can understand religious people not feeling comfortable with having abortions; however, I think it's sinful to continue to procreate when you have the power to avoid the pregnancy if you can't afford to take care of your children. It's not Christlike to be a burden to others.

There's a television show called "Bar Rescue," with Jon Taffer as the businessman who goes into failing bars and helps turn them around financially. It's amazing to see how people who are in hundreds of thousands of dollars of debt argue with Taffer because their egos get in the way and they don't want to change. Often, the bar owners know they're wrong; however, some of them would rather fail than listen to the advice of someone else. Taffer is animated and he yells and screams at the owners. For the owners who listen to him, their bars have a high rate of becoming money makers.

I have watched Trump crash and burn because of some of the things he'd say and I wished he had a Taffer who was able to tame his ego. While speaking at a rally, Trump said, "Hillary wants to abolish essentially the 2nd Amendment. By the way, if she gets to pick her judges, nothing you can do folks. Although the second Amendment people, maybe there is, I don't know." I knew he'd stepped in the poop again with this comment. The media spin said Trump was encouraging someone to shoot Hillary. Trump said he meant the 2nd Amendment people would make the difference by voting.

I was disappointed with Trump because I felt he should've focused more on the Democratic National Committee emails that WikiLeaks released that spoke about racist things Democrats said, and I wanted him to stick to speaking about the Clinton Foundation and focus on the changes he would like to make as president.

A friend said to me, "Trump's mouth is going to get us into a war."

"Maybe countries would respect us more if Trump was president. Inaction can also get us into a war," I said.

"That's ignorant!"

I was willing to listen to her views without saying her views were ignorant; however, she wasn't willing to do the same for me. What I said is also possible. She thought about it and instead of agreeing, she had to say "ignorant."

In January 2016, hours before Obama gave his State of the Union Address, American Navy men were on a ship and they were captured by Iranians. Our soldiers were forced on their knees with their hands behind their backs. Neither John Kerry, Secretary of State, nor Obama publicly demeaned Iran for the poor treatment of our soldiers. Presidents Reagan, Clinton and both Bushes would've made a public comment to let Iran know their behavior wasn't acceptable. A President Trump would've let Iran know they'd better get their act together.

Lately, it seems like Trump's new campaign manager Kellyanne Conway has done a good job of helping to tame him. He's becoming more likeable and his poll numbers are rising.

Chapter 24

Disappearing Loyalty Pledge

The Republican presidential loyalty pledge stated: I affirm that if I do not win the 2016 Republican nomination for president of the United States, I will endorse the 2016 Republican presidential nominee, regardless of who it is. I further pledge that I will not seek to run as an independent or write-in candidate, nor will I seek or accept the nomination for president of any other party. This pledge was all about trying to trap Donald Trump into publicly not keeping his word. Republican presidential candidates didn't think Trump would win the primary, so they wanted to keep him from running as an independent because they were sure he wouldn't win the Republican primary. Surprise! Trump won the 2016 presidential Republican nomination. All of the candidates agreed to sign the loyalty pledge, however, some of the main candidates who called Trump a crybaby and immature are some of the same men who refused to honor the loyalty pledge.

What a lady Carly Fiorina was. She endorsed Trump for president because she thought he's a better choice than Hillary. She's a big woman for doing so. She signed the pledge and she kept her word. This decision was probably difficult since Trump made negative remarks about her face. Her integrity makes her beautiful! Ben Carson, Marco Rubio, Jim Gilmore, Chris Christie, Rick Santorum, Rand Paul, Mike Huckabee and Rick Perry have all kept their loyalty promise and endorsed Trump. Jeb Bush, Lindsey Graham and John Kasich are some who refused to endorse Trump. They are little boys for not honoring the pledge.

Mitt Romney's behavior was beyond nasty when he went public to denounce Trump. He actually had a press conference to dis him. He said, "Donald Trump is a phony and a fraud." It was embarrassing to hear Romney speak his selected words because in the past he came across as a distinguished man. I once thought he was a decent man. I pray Trump wins so that Romney could learn that his behavior was worse than Trump's. Romney didn't condemn Hillary at the rate he condemned Trump. I think this is a case of jealousy. The biggest fear with Republicans who don't support Trump is the possibility that if he becomes president he can become one of the best presidents we've had. Career politicians have a difficult time accepting that a loud, bombastic businessman can win the presidency because this makes them fearful of more non-politicians coming in taking their positions. Romney hasn't gotten over losing the 2012 presidential election to Obama. Romney publicly tried to minimize his wealth and Trump publicly boasted about his. Trump is more authentic than Romney.

There are politicians who agree with Trump on having a temporary ban on Muslims coming to the United States from terrorist countries, but they are afraid to admit it publicly. If politicians cared about protecting Americans, they should all be in harmony with a temporary ban until we fix our broken immigration system. Instead, they bash Trump's suggestion as racist.

Trump is still considered a racist for saying he didn't believe Obama wasn't born in the United States. However, Trump also questioned the birthright of Ted Cruz because he was born in Calgary, Canada. His mother is American and his father is Cuban. Though Trump publicly doubted Cruz's citizenship, people still call him a racist for thinking Obama was born in Kenya. Trump is an equal opportunity doubter. If Trump doubted a white person or any race person's citizenship he would publicly say it.

Trump would be the best president for the black community because he can use his business dealings to bring manufacturing jobs and other jobs to inner cities. I would trust Trump to bring jobs to the black communities before I would Hillary.

Instead of Republicans saying Trump is a Democrat, they should get smart and realize he's their best bet for having a Republican president. With the demographics changing in America, and Democrats convincing millions of people that the Republicans are racists and bigots, Republicans like Ted Cruz who is religiously rigid about birth control, abortions and gay rights will have a difficult time becoming president today. Some Republicans can't see it; however, Trump is their best hope. People can attempt to minimize Trump's accomplishments; however, what he has accomplished is "yuge." He knocked down 17 career politicians and he got more votes than any other Republican in the primary. This created envy with his adversaries.

Trump has given millions of people their voices back—especially white people because they were so afraid of the politically correct police calling them racists and bigots because they are unhappy about their communities, schools, jobs and neighborhoods deteriorating because of illegal immigration.

Ben Carson was correct when he said Republicans wrote off the black vote. I think they haven't put emphasis on the black communities because they didn't think they were an important voting bloc since black people represent only 13% of America's population. Republicans should be able to list several accomplishments they're responsible for in the black communities, not only because they want the black vote, but because it's their job. Trump waited too long to solicit the black vote. Speaking about black people, Trump asked, "What do you have to lose?" Instead of enforcing the negative, he should've implanted the positive and say, "Here's what you have to 'gain' with Trump."

During Trump's immigration speech in Phoenix, he said, "We decide who comes to America." This made a lot of Americans happy because we feel like we've been the abandoned stepchildren in America. Recently, there was a video from the southern border. Illegal immigrants trying to cross the border told our border patrol officers, "Obama said we can come." It's shameful that our politicians are sending out invitations by not enforcing our immigration laws to illegal immigrants to come to our country illegally. Trump's bold stance on illegal immigration made many Americans feel validated.

Some people say Trump is too simple. Sometimes his simplicity is wisdom. When asked about North Carolina's law saying transgender people must use the restroom that correlates with their sex at birth, Trump said, "Transgender people can use whatever bathroom they want." He said transgender Caitlyn Jenner can use whatever bathroom she wants to use at Trump Towers. He said the restroom transgenders choose to use is fine the way it is. I agree!

Chapter 25

Thank You Obama!!!

Some say the media scrutiny around Hillary's health was unfair. When she seemed to faint after leaving a 9/11 celebration, I wondered if her fall was also symbolic of her falling in the polls, which could cause her to lose the election. Sen. John McCain's health was scrutinized more than Hillary's when he ran for president in 2008. There was a commercial showing a picture of McCain with a bandage on his face that was covering a scar he had from his cancer surgery in 2000. He was 72 years old when he ran for the presidency. In the commercial, the doctor said, "The relevance of knowing the details of his course with melanoma are very important. Another bout of cancer would profoundly impact his capacity to lead." People weren't called sexist for publicly mentioning McCain's health.

If a commercial was made today showing Hillary coughing and appearing to faint and fall, this ad would be considered sexist. Regardless of male or female, our candidates for president should have to show their health records to the American people. We have the right to know that we are voting in a healthy candidate. Trump was on the Dr. Oz show and he admitted he's overweight. It would be sexist to some to ask how much Hillary weighs. Obesity is also a major health issue that cause health costs to rise.

Lately, Trump has been Trumping Hillary. She was invited to Mexico to speak; however, Trump beat her and took advantage of the opportunity. Hillary didn't go to Louisiana when they had people dying from the floods. 40,000 homes were affected and 30,000 people were removed from cars and homes. This flood has been one of the worst United States disasters since Hurricane Sandy. Some people felt Hillary didn't show up because Louisiana isn't a battleground state for her like Ohio and Pennsylvania. Trump visited the flood victims and he looked presidential. Obama elected to stay at Martha's Vineyard and golf. He's on his way out of office so he didn't need to show up either. Hillary and Obama, like all politicians, pick and choose which poor people they want to publicly show empathy toward.

I was watching Hillary on television speak at a rally in North Carolina. This was her first public appearance since her doctor gave her orders to take a few days off from campaigning. She stepped off the steps of the airplane deliberately. Her eyes had the appearance of someone who was heavily medicated. Though she tried to look strong and in control, her movements were jagged. When l had pneumonia I felt uncoordinated when I didn't take the necessary time off to rest. I was really trying to listen to Hillary's voice but it was too harsh so I turned the volume down. I enjoy hearing our presidents speak; however, hearing Hillary's non-emotional, dull speeches for four years or more would not be pleasant for me. I've heard many people say that her voice and the way she speaks turns them off. Bill Clinton, back in the day, was an awesome communicator who connected with people. Maybe his dirty deeds have caught up with him because his magic is gone, and when he speaks now I turn the volume down. Chelsea Clinton's aura is better and more authentic than her parents.

Hillary said that it hits her in the gut when a little girl comes up to her and tells her she's afraid of being deported. If this hits her in the gut, she should want to secure our borders and immediately send illegal immigrants back to their countries. This should encourage her to want to end the anchor baby policy. She brags about her foreign policy knowledge; however, she has a poor performance with securing our southern borders. Security and protecting Americans is a security issue regardless if it's in America or abroad. She doesn't talk about securing our borders because she wants more brown people to enter America illegally so she and Democrats can dominate the White House. It's interesting how the Australian government isn't called racist for their strict immigration laws. Their politicians realized that massive immigration was affecting the welfare and jobs for their citizens. They're putting their citizens first.

Remaining in a marriage with a cheating spouse is a personal choice; however, many people think Hillary stayed married to Bill for the sake of power and to be able to use his influence to run for president.

I didn't vote for Obama; however, I am happy that he won because many Americans think race, gender and the political affiliation of a person dictates their character. This is far from the truth. Many black people are unhappy with Obama because they felt he hasn't made improvements in black communities. He has spent more time on helping illegal immigrants and refugees than he has on improving black communities. If he wanted to help black communities with better schooling, housing and safer neighborhoods, he wouldn't be supportive of amnesty. When it comes to Obama, some black people hear Janet Jackson's song, "What Have You Done for Me Lately?" play in their head. My black friend said, "I am unhappy with Obama because I feel he let black people down, but I don't let the white man know how I feel." She then said, "And I don't talk bad about black people to white people."

I said, "Well, white people are aware that unemployment, housing costs and crime is higher in the black communities since Obama has been in office, and by the way, they see news reports about black on black crime on the six o' clock news." There are some black people who don't think much of me because I didn't pick up my pom-poms and cheer out of excitement for Obama. I need more than race, gender and party affiliation to be moved. According to www.thehill.com, from 2009 to 2014, black incomes fell more than any other racial or ethnic group.

In 2004, when Obama spoke at the Democratic National Convention, many people were blown away with his style of speaking. Some said they were reminded of Dr. Martin Luther King and they were waiting to hear him say, "I have a dream." I didn't feel what many felt with his DNC speech. Obama is a head speaker. When he speaks, in his aura I see the energy centered around his head rather than his heart. When Dr. Martin Luther King spoke, his energy was centered in his heart area. Back in the day when Bill Clinton was "sexy Bill", he had a large purple aura and he had a way of making you think his words came from his heart. Bill was an eloquent speaker whether he was speaking from a teleprompter or not.

When Obama isn't speaking from a teleprompter, he sounds like a different speaker and he blunders a lot. Trump's most authentic way of communicating is when he's uncensored and shoots from his hip; however, it gets him into trouble with the politically correct police. Trump's lesson is to learn to use words from his gut with a softer lens. I had to learn this lesson too. Today, I am comfortable with my voice and instead of focusing on the words I say, I am more concerned with the place where my words stem from because I bridge them with my gut sensor and my heart center.

A Trump win would mean a blow to Obama's ego. He despises Trump because Trump said he was the worst president we've ever had and Trump would make an effort to undo some of his policies and revamp Obamacare and, create programs to help thousands of veterans who are treated poorly by our government. Osama bin Laden was killed under Obama's presidency; however, I think his biggest accomplishment has been making America browner by tying the hands of ICE (Immigration Customs Enforcement) and our border patrol agents from enforcing our immigration laws and publicly supporting amnesty.

Obama was angry when the Muslim 14-year-old boy was arrested for building a clock that looked like a bomb; however, a seven-year-old boy in Baltimore was suspended because he chewed his Pop Tart in the shape of a gun. Obama spoke publicly about the Muslim boy and invited him to the White House to show off his clock. Facebook founder Mark Zuckerberg invited the Muslim teenager to visit him and Twitter offered him an internship. Chewing a Pop Tart into a gun is also creative, however Pop Tart gun boy is white and all he received was a suspension. If the Pop Tart boy was black or Muslim, this would've been called a case of racism.

Chapter 26

Burn City Burn

My biggest disappointment with Obama has been his alignment with Black Lives Matter. The president of the United States did not publicly denounce a group who chants in the street, "Pigs in a blanket! Fry 'em like bacon!" Just as Trump should've readily denounced the KKK, I think Obama, Hillary, Trump and all politicians should have denounced Black Lives Matter. At a rally outside the 2016 Democratic National Convention there was a Black Lives Matter protest. A black woman standing on the back of a pickup truck yelled to the crowd through a megaphone, "White media get to the back! Black media come to the front." She yelled at a white man, "Excuse me sir, somebody needs to tell this person to get to the back. Go. Somebody needs to tell these folks to get to the back. This is a black brown resistance march."

Can you imagine Dr. Martin Luther King aligning himself with a group that wouldn't want white people, black people and all races of people up front and present at his rallies to create equality? White people being present can minimize the idea that all white people are racist. King was a change agent, not a divider. He was an example of how he wanted others to treat him by having grace with how he dealt with people regardless of their race.

If the Tea Party, or any group, publicly said they wanted cops, presidents or any other people's lives taken, there should be some kind of criminal charges filed against them or anyone who would do such. Poor behavior shouldn't be excused because of your race, gender or political affiliation.

I was disappointed that we had a black sitting president who didn't go into the inner cities and speak to the people and ask for calm before riots started and in the midst of riots. His silence was dangerous. I like Milwaukee County Sheriff Joe Clark because he's not afraid to call black people out on their poor behavior. He would make an awesome president because he doesn't use a person's race as an excuse for their poor behavior. Clark said, "Democrats took blacks from the cotton field to the plantation called, 'The Ghetto.'" I agree with him. It's unfortunate that if a white person said the same thing it's considered racist.

Whenever Black Lives Matter chants in the street, "No justice no peace," they're actually causing their own people more harm. The "no peace" will mainly come as a result of police officers not wanting to be as involved when poor law-abiding citizens call for emergency police assistance when they're being attacked by their own race. When I was a police office and we felt we were targets, we'd slow down when answering a violent call and we'd hope that the violence would've subsided by the time we arrived since we were already targets. Black Lives Matter threatening chants causes more fatalities and injuries with the very lives of the people they claim lives matter.

When I heard Black Lives Matter's violent, destructive chants, I knew they would cause crime in the black communities to rise because of police apathy. A year after the formation of Black Lives Matter, crime has gone up as much as 70% in some inner-city neighborhoods. Since January 2016, (less than a year) 3,000 people have been shot in the south side of Chicago and 472 have been killed. Someone said to me, "The

ACLU has an app for black people to use to video the police when they stop you."

My question was, "Where's the app for black people to use for when they're being attacked by black people?" I think the ACLU app is a good idea, however, too many black people think the police are their enemy when their biggest enemy is their own race of criminals harming them. By no means am I defending police officers who commit criminal acts on citizens. Any police officer who unlawfully violates a citizen in any way should be punished. When I worked as a police officer in Miami it was difficult dealing with inner city black people who had no desire in life but to be criminals and cause harm towards their own people. It's a tougher job than ever being a police officer today. Police officers still have to protect while they serve with targets on their backs.

It's depressing for black police officers to see generations of their people hanging out on street corners using drugs and abusing alcohol. Sometimes I saw great-grandfathers, grandfathers, fathers and sons all sitting together outside run-down store fronts where people were abusing drug and alcohol. Though there was little to no desire from many of the people in these kinds of neighborhoods to change their lives, I still protected them the way I would a rich, white law-abiding citizen or any other race person. The majority of my fellow police officers felt the same way. There were also good, law-abiding black citizens who couldn't afford to move out of some of the crime-laden neighborhoods. Ninety-three percent of homicides of black people are caused by black people. If Black Lives Matter, we need to start showing ourselves, each other and the world by not killing and harming each other.

Black Lives Matter says black lives matter; however, they seem to only care about the life of a black person when their life is taken by a white person. Black

Lives Matter didn't seem to matter much when gang bangers would kill their own race for wearing their gang colors. Black mothers and fathers were afraid for their children to wear red and blue clothing because of the Crips blue gang color and the Bloods red gang color, because people were killed for wearing their colors. Little black children were denied the right to enjoy being pulled down the street safely in a red wagon. This treatment was worse than any modern-day racism by the white man. Actress Roseanne Barr said she has black men in her family and she's afraid for their safety because of cops killing black men. I've heard black mothers say the same. They should relax their fear of the white man killing their black loved ones because the chances of them being killed or hurt by another black person is much, much higher.

I am disappointed with politicians or anyone who thinks they need to apologize for saying "All Lives Matter." Some black people think it's racist to say "All Lives Matter." Until we all collectively respect our own individual lives and the lives of our brothers and sisters regardless of their race, we're going to continue to be divided. Because of the mistreatment of black people in America, we should be the group who treats each other better than any other race. Instead, we treat each other the worst and then we expect people to believe us when we chant Black Lives Matter. Years ago, in Los Angeles there were flyers circulating that said: The black gang bangers have taken the KKK'S job of killing niggers away from them. Some black people had the audacity to be angry about the flyers at a time when gang members killed their own people daily.

When I was a police officer in Miami, there was a program called "Officer Friendly." This program brought police officers and the communities together to work out misunderstandings and problems. The program helped to improve the relationship between the police and inner cities. Our president and all politicians should be instrumental in assisting police departments with these kinds of programs. If I said I was always the good one in my relationships, and the people I was involved with were always the bad ones, I would be lying. When there's conflict, both sides must look at their participation. Black people can't expect for police to change their behavior if they don't change theirs. Black people need to learn to respect the police just as the police need to respect black people and all race people.

Chapter 27

Your "Fro" Doesn't make you a "Bro"

Is San Francisco 49er football quarterback Colin Kaepernick really angry about being benched? Is his protest really about saying that the 49ers franchise is racist because he's been a bench warmer? Did his activism start to brew because a white quarterback, Blane Gabbert, is the starting quarterback for the 49ers?

Colin Kaepernick refused to stand during the opening of his team's football game when the national anthem was played. He said his reasons are, "I am not going to stand up to show pride in a flag for a country that oppresses black people and people of color. To me, this is bigger than football and it would be selfish on my part to look the other way. There are bodies in the street and people getting paid leave and getting away with murder." He also said, "You have Hillary who has called black teens or black kids super-predators, you have Donald Trump who's openly racist. We have a presidential candidate who has deleted emails and done things illegally and is a presidential candidate. That doesn't make sense to me because if that was any other person, you'd be in prison. So, what is this country really standing for?"

I wonder if Kaepernick is only speaking about dead bodies in the streets that are a result of black men being killed by white police officers or if he's also speaking about the thousands of black men and women who are killed by their own people. I wonder how he feels about a sitting black president who hasn't done more to help curb the violence in the south side of Chicago and other crime-ridden inner cities. I wonder how he feels about a sitting black president who puts more energy into helping and assisting illegal immigrants and refugees more than he does poor black inner-city people.

All police shootings should be investigated. A video recording doesn't always show every minor detail or the full occurrence. As a police officer, there are times when you have a fraction of a second to make a decision that may save your life. The video recording that showed Rodney King who was beaten severely by police was obviously an excessive police brutality case and it was a wonder King lived afterwards. Most of the police shootings aren't clear cut to me because of my experience as a police officer. I am able to see both sides. I think there are some bad, corrupt police officers; however, I think they are the minority.

It may be helpful for Kaepernick to do some research about history and our world today and maybe he'll understand more of why America is the way it is. Stuff is happening all over the world and it will continue to happen. The world has changed and it's changed drastically. There are breakdowns in the family. There was a time in the black family where the elders were looked up to and respected. Today, in my family and many families, the elders are taken advantage of. If parents didn't give their adult children and relatives money, they wouldn't get a visit from them.

Maybe if Kaepernick had an understanding of spirituality, he'd understand more of why things are happening the way they are. Everything happens to give us an opportunity to do something about it. We can choose to be a part of change by helping the healing process or we can come up with options that fuel the fire and cause more division. His response to white police officers killing black men is to choose not to honor the American flag and stand for the national anthem. Because I was a police officer, I honor the flag. Maybe Kaepernick isn't aware of the white people and other people who are killed by police. America isn't perfect; however, I honor and give thanks for the opportunity to be in this country where I am allowed to have a platform to speak my truths and have a platform to create change. Honoring the flag and standing for a national anthem that represents this great country is a small price to pay for the many opportunities I've been granted in America. When I honor the flag, I am honoring the platform I have to create to help make changes in my personal life and my country.

When I am honoring our flag, as a woman, I think about how proud I am to live in America where I don't have to live under radical Sharia Law, Islamic laws and rules. I am thankful and grateful for my fore-parents who fought so dearly to pave a way for me today. Because I am thankful and grateful for the many sacrifices that my fore-parents made, I make an effort not to harm my fellow man, especially my black brothers and sisters. I know the pain and suffering we've endured for hundreds of years at the hands of white people and black people.

I was listening to radio talk show host Larry Elder on the radio and he was speaking about times in America when his parents were young. If his mother went to a store to buy a dress, she had to make sure it would be her proper size, because once a black person touched an item they had to buy it. He said his father tried on a hat in a store one day and he had to buy it because it had been touched by a black man's head. His father went to court to apply for a license to have a car service that transported people. In court, the white judge denied his father the license because his white friend wanted the business and he called his father a nigger in court. They didn't use their past experiences of racism to forbid them from recognizing that there were also wonderful things for them to be a part of in America.

America isn't perfect; however, we've come a long way. I like what former San Francisco 49er Jerry Rice said about Kaepernick. "All lives matter. So much going on in this world today. Can we all just get along! Colin, I respect your stance but don't disrespect the flag." I also liked what former NBA star Shaquille O'Neal had to say. "To each his own. I don't really have a lot to say on it but I would never do that. My father was a military man, and you know, he protected this country. Uncles are in law enforcement, you know, they go out and work hard every day." Shaq said he wondered why Kaepernick has waited till now to protest and didn't protest during the Ferguson protest.

Maybe Kaepernick would think differently if the media showed the amount of white people and other race people who were killed by police. There are some bad doctors and nurses. However, I think there are also some good quality doctors and nurses. I wouldn't want to punish the entire medical profession because some doctors' and nurses' negligence have caused patients to die. If there was a nationwide movement to cause doctors and nurses harm because of the poor treatment by some, they wouldn't give us the best service because they wouldn't feel compelled to help save people who want to kill them. The people who need doctors and nurses the most wouldn't get proper care. Kaepernick wore socks with pigs dressed as cops. This would be the same as wearing socks with pigs dressed in doctors' and nurses' uniforms if you wanted to protest them because some doctors and nurses were responsible for some people's deaths that were due to malpractice. The amount of lives people in the medical profession save is greater than the amount of lives they lose. I feel the same way about our police officers.

I wonder if Kaepernick thinks that black people also have a responsibility to change their behavior and respect the police. I find it difficult to believe that black people who kill and assault their own would have respectful manners when they are stopped or accosted by the police. When there's conflict, you must look at the behavior of all involved. Regardless of how much training a police officer has, they are only human. It's possible that they are more apt to use violence quicker when they interact with black men than they do with other races because of how violent some black people are with each other. This may cause some police to react faster when making a life-or-death decision.

The most interesting thing about Kaepernick's activism is that there are some black people who don't accept him as black. His biological mother is white and his biological father is black. Black people are more apt to accept Obama as black because his skin is darker. Because of Kaepernick's light skin color, some black people don't accept him as one of theirs, even though he sports a gigantic afro.

A black woman said to me, "White police officers kill black men because it only takes a high school education to become a police officer." She was insinuating that a college degree or a Ph.D. would determine how someone would respond emotionally in a life-or-death situation. I would like to think I'd remain cool, calm and collected if I was in an emergency situation where my life could be taken. Regardless of the amount of training I may have, I can't guarantee what I may or may not think or do in an emergency, and I wouldn't know what past traumas and fears may be triggered. When I was in the police academy I was having trouble getting a 200 passing score on the firearm shooting test. I would squeeze the trigger slowly, however, my hands would jerk and my bullets would miss the target. I had to have a session with a psychiatrist to get to the bottom of what was causing me to not pass. The psychiatrist asked me what were my earliest memories of hearing loud, frightful noises that caused me to panic.

When I was a child I went to my grandfather's funeral and the screaming, shouting and fainting scared me. The psychiatrist said the anticipation of the noise from the gun firing caused me to lose my composure and that caused me to jerk my hand that held the firearm. I'd miss the target because my past fear of the trauma from my grandfather's funeral was triggered. He helped me to feel comfortable about visiting my old painful memory, I cried and released it. The doctor then played meditation music and gave me positive affirmations to replace the old traumatic emotions I had stored and suppressed in my subconscious. A week later, I passed my firearm test and I became a sharpshooter. Regardless of how many college degrees one may have, it's possible that certain people and situations can trigger our old wounds and cause us to panic.

When I first heard about Kaepernick refusing to stand for our flag, I was unhappy. I had a conversation with myself and I had to accept his way of using his right to protest in America, just as I appreciate my right to protest my way. My public speaking, writing, and, my books are my ways of protesting what I think needs to change. There was an older black man on the news speaking about how he and other black youths protested in the sixties. He complained about black male thugs who riot, loot and create violence when a police officer kills a black person. He said, "Today they don't wear shirts, they wear sagging pants when they protest. We wore white shirts, black ties and black pants. We were organized and protested in a peaceful way." If black protests were carried out this way today, people of all races would feel more comfortable to be a part.

Lack of gratitude is one of the reasons there's so much unhappiness and so many problems in our world. Though Kaepernick has a right to protest however he wants to, I am concerned about young black people adopting his attitude and dismissing all the wonderful things that have happened and are happening in America. His attitude can encourage young people to go through life being victims and not victors because there is no country where everything is perfect. In countries where everyone is basically the same race, there are still problems. I think Kaepernick has a lot of personal, internal issues going on and his problems are bigger than not standing and saluting our flag.

I am grateful to Kaepernick, because on a spiritual level he was chosen to ignite American pride. Some liberals made you feel guilty about having American pride and chanting USA! USA! I don't think he was prepared for the backlash he received. We needed Kaepernick to ignite American pride after years of Obama publicly dissing us. Kaepernick motivated me to purchase a dress with the print of the American flag. Everyone and everything is a symbol. Kaepernick was the stand-in for Americans to remember how much they love this great country, and they stood up and said, "You may not love her ... but we do."

Chapter 28

Who Killed Chivalry?

Often, we are the problem that we complain about. We don't like to see our shadow side, our dark side, because we pride ourselves on being good. We like to think it's always the other person who's creating havoc in our lives because we want to think we are good, Godly people. Regardless of how much God you may think you have inside of you, we all have some "shadiness" inside of us too. Lord knows I have some skeletons dancing in my closet! Because some people's closet skeletons rattle louder than others doesn't mean we don't all have them.

An observant elderly woman was riding on the long-term parking airport bus. A man asked me if he could help me with my bags, and I said, "Thank you but I can handle them."

When I sat next to the elderly woman, she said to me, "Honey, when I ride this bus I often hear you women refuse to let men help you with your bags, and when they offer you their seat on the crowded bus you tell them no, yet women complain about men not being gentlemen anymore."

The elderly woman was correct, and she made me recognize where I too was part of a situation I had complained about. Of course, I can handle my own bags; however, I had to be accepting of someone who wanted to assist me. I became more aware of accepting what appeared to be small acts of kindness from people. I open and hold doors for men and women. Notice I said "appeared" to be small acts of kindness because when someone is kind to you, it's always a big deal. We create change when we become the solution to the problems we complain about. One by one we can create great change. It's a lack of integrity to be *that* which we claim we don't like or appreciate.

It's beyond hypocritical for black people to only care about white police officers killing black people when thousands more are being killed by the hands of their own people. Some of the very black people who protest, riot and loot because a white police officer kills a black man have assaulted black people. If white people were going into black neighborhoods shooting and killing thousands of black people yearly, there would be a major media outcry about racism in America. However, this problem is often ignored because it's black on black crime.

When I speak about this, some black people say black on black crime is propaganda. Many poor, law-abiding black people who think they're trapped in these crime-ridden neighborhoods because they're poor, don't think the homicides and assaults are propaganda in their neighborhoods. In one month, August 2016, there were 90 people killed in the inner cities in Chicago.

Professional basketball player Dwayne Wade's cousin, who was the mother of four, was shot and killed while pushing her baby down the street in Chicago. Her story made the media because of Wade's celebrity status, however, there are thousands of more black victims who are killed and assaulted by their own people whose stories don't make the media. Who is going to protest for these mothers and fathers of dead children? A couple of weeks ago there was an elderly black man who was watering his lawn when some thugs came along and shot and killed him. It's common for shootings to occur every few hours in Chicago.

Thugs in Chicago hitch up their waistbands insinuating they have guns when police drive by. Police have to ignore this kind of behavior because they don't won't to excite the tension already in the crime-ridden areas. There was a time police wouldn't have ignored such. With the media attention about "only" black people being killed by white police; the police are apprehensive. There needs to be a movement like Black Lives Matter that teach black people how to respect the police. If you want to wave a gun (fake or real) or knife at the police, there are going to be serious consequences. The National Guard may have to intervene to help the uncontrollable crime in Chicago.

When you defend and enable poor behavior, it comes back and bites you in the butt. This is happening now in many crime-ridden black communities. Until this level of threat spreads to wealthy white neighborhoods, there will continue to be a rise in black on black crime. When the police try to do their job, they're called "racist," so they've backed off and have allowed the inner cities to run amok.

Black people can be proud of Obama because he's a black president; however, what good has his skin color done for them in cities like Chicago? The president represents the nation's father and it's difficult for black people to accept their own don't give a damn about them. Chicago is the president's former home town and he dismissed black people by not doing something about the crime in their communities. When Obama publicly reprimanded black men for not supporting their families, some black people were offended. He was also reprimanded for calling black rioters and looters criminals and thugs for rioting in Baltimore. Obama avoids calling out black people with poor behavior because he wanted to leave office with high approval ratings. As long as politicians can pimp the black vote simply because they're Democrats, conditions in black neighborhoods won't change.

There are many black people who are racist. I know a black woman who thinks all white people are racist. She volunteered to help take care of an elderly, sick white woman who lived in her condominium. When the woman died, she made the black woman her beneficiary and she left her ownership of her condo which was valued close to $200,000. I said to the black woman, "How can you still say all white people are racist when this white woman was kind to you?"

"Because white people are the devil." She added, "I don't share this story with people." She doesn't share this story because she enjoys going through life trying to convince herself and others that all white people are racist. This kind act makes it difficult for her to hate all white people. She admitted the white neighbor was kind to her and treated her better than her relatives treated her.

Chapter 29

Captain Offends a Sista

Kim Kardashian was going inside a medical building in California and a white teenager yelled out, "Nigger lover." Kanye West, her husband, was offended and said, "We've got enough money to buy our own island or some shit. I'll be damned if I raise my daughter around ignorance and flat-out blatant racism." Many white people have bought Kanye and Kim's products, which enables them to purchase their own island. There will always be some kind of "isms" because we are human. Sometimes black people call people and situations racist when it's possible that the situation isn't based on racism. Maybe the white teenager was jealous of Kanye, he has a beautiful wife and like he said, he has enough money to buy his own island. Maybe the white teenager was pissed off because females he's attracted to want to be in relationships with black males. Maybe it was about money and the teenager intentionally wanted to set Kanye off. If it was about money, the teenager succeeded because Kanye physically attacked him. TMZ reported he had to pay a settlement of $250,000 to the teenager.

Jackson Hole, Wyoming has only a handful of black people. I was there once and a white woman told me about her black Jamaican male friends who said they won't go back to Jackson Hole because of the racist white people who stared at them. She informed her friends, "Oh no, when you guys left, many people came up to me and complimented your good looks. They said you guys look exotic and you have nice muscular bodies."

"Oh," they responded.

I have a white female friend who is married to a black man. They have a son and a daughter. She said to me, "I get so pissed off when my family and I go to restaurants and malls because racist people stare at us."

"If I saw you and your family I would stare at you too. Are you aware of how beautiful and exotic looking you and your family are? Your children are stunning!"

"You know, I'd never thought about it that way," she said.

The majority of situations that people call racism are not racism. Black people are notorious for defending other black people's poor behavior, and this perpetuates poor behavior. A black woman said to me, "Can you believe the way they're treating Bill Cosby with these rape allegations? They're only doing this to him because he's black."

"He admitted to drugging and having sex with a woman in a deposition," I said.

"I know but that was supposed to remain sealed." This woman was more concerned about a black man's reputation than with having him convicted for crimes. It's interesting how some black people ran to the rescue of O.J. Simpson when he was accused of murder and Michael Jackson when he was accused of molesting children, because they are two black men who made it obvious that they wanted to be saturated with white people.

Years ago, a coworker said, "Have you heard the company is being racist and trying to fire black employees?"

"Are these the same black coworkers who don't show up for work and don't make the effort to call the company to let them know they aren't showing up? Are these the same black coworkers who are often late for work and have missed several days of work?"

"You're right. I know my friend Wanda was fired, but she called out sick a lot."

"Well I know some white coworkers who got fired for the same poor behavior." The company was firing people based on poor performance, not race. There are many gay and ethnic people who get away with more because they file discriminatory lawsuits. One rude, unprofessional coworker said, "The company can't fire me because I'm black, gay, and bipolar." This doesn't mean that there aren't any discriminatory practices in companies. However, there are some situations that aren't based on race.

Black people are quick to call someone racist; however, we do a fine job of mistreating each other. We say things and treat each other in some of the same poor ways that a white person may treat us. We accept the poor behavior when it's black on black however when it's black vs. white we cry racism. I was an assistant at a trade show with a black female sales rep. Her white male boss said to her, "You look like Whoopi Goldberg."

"Just so you are aware, when someone tells a black woman they look like Whoopi Goldberg or Oprah Winfrey, we don't take that as a compliment." She flounced away.

"Ce Ce, I am so sorry. I didn't mean any harm. I didn't mean to offend her. I don't think Whoopi or Oprah is unattractive," her boss said.

"Don't worry about it. It's a black thing." The man was sorry for his comment. Though Whoopi and Oprah are both successful, smart women, they are often put down by black people because of how they look. It's okay for black people to demean each other however it's called racism if a white person does the same.

Black people are sensitive when people make unflattering comments about the way Michelle Obama looks; however, they seem to have forgotten about how awful first lady Barbara Bush was treated. My black coworker was angry because a white coworker said Michelle Obama was ugly. I asked her, "Have you forgotten the names people publicly called Barbara Bush?" She was called old, wrinkly and some said she looked like a pilgrim and George Washington. It wasn't considered racist if a black person made fun of her appearance.

"I can't talk about this. I am too upset," my black friend said.

When Chelsea Clinton was young, people publicly spoke about how ugly she was. In 1998, Sen. John McCain, who is angry with Trump for saying he isn't a war hero, asked, "Why is Chelsea (Clinton) so ugly?"

When Bill Clinton was president, conservative talk show host Rush Limbaugh said there was a White House cat named Socks and there was a White House dog named Chelsea. Imagine a radio host saying the same about Obama's daughters. If the same was said about Obama's daughters, the radio host would've quickly gotten a pink slip.

There was a cartoon in the Washington Post that depicted Ted Cruz with two ropes connecting him to his daughters that were images of monkeys. Ladies and gentlemen, can you imagine a cartoonist making an image of Obama's daughters as monkeys? This would've been called the ultimate racist act. That cartoonist probably wouldn't have been able to get a job again. I didn't hear black people being offended by this being done to Cruz's daughters, though.

Some said it was racist for the Russian Tennis Federation President to call Venus and Serena Williams "The Williams brothers." He was banned for a year and had to pay a $25,000 fine. Years ago, a white man asked me if I was a woman because he said my legs were muscular. Whether he meant for his comment to be racist didn't matter to me because I'd been working out and I was proud of my toned, muscular legs. Maybe he was jealous because I had more muscles in my legs than he had in his girly legs.

George W. Bush was the most publicly verbally beaten up president. He was called dumb, stupid and ignorant and it was always just dandy with the politically correct police to dump on Bush. There weren't any limits. Some black people think Obama has been treated worse. I ask them, "Are you aware that people had mocked funerals for Bush?"

"Really?"

People have called all of our presidents' derogatory names. Sometimes it's just the nature of how Americans treat their politicians. These are a few of the names they were called. Obama was called Captain Clueless, jack ass in charge and of course, nigger. George W. Bush was called smirking chimp and Dumbya,

They surely would've known if people had mocked funerals for Obama because it would've been spewed all over the news as "racism." During a joint congressional hearing, a politician pointed at Obama and called him a liar. When black people mention this, I ask if they think it was worse when George W. Bush was booed while giving a state of the union address. Can you imagine if this happened to Obama? Lawdy, lawdy Miss Clawdy! This would've been the biggest racist story of the century. All of these behaviors are poor. I may not like politicians' policies; however, I respect their positions as our presidents and politicians.

Some black people didn't pay much attention to the media spin about presidents and politicians until a black man became president. They are convinced that white Republicans have tried to stop and block everything that Obama has tried to accomplish because he's black.

The purpose of the Democratic and Republican parties is to have checks and balances, though they often allow politics to get in the way of making the best decision for the people. When Sen. Mitch O'Connell publicly said the Republicans were going to do whatever they could to block Obama, this gave some the impression that this was happening because the president was black. Democrats and Republicans do the same to each other regardless of the race of the president. It's called politics.

For eight years when George W. Bush was president, I had to hear about how much people hated him. It was open season on Bush. If someone stubbed their big toe, it was Bush's fault. People were deaf mutes when it came to speaking about Obama in a negative way because they were afraid of being called racist. One of the benefits of having a white (especially) Republican president, is that you can disagree with their policies and you won't have to be concerned with being called a racist. If Trump becomes president, people will be back to openly saying how much they hate our president.

Again, the way you right a wrong is to take a stand regardless of what the sex, race, gender or political affiliation a person is. If you don't like someone calling politicians that you like derogatory names, then you shouldn't be an offender of the same with other politicians because you disagree with them. When I tell people this who boldly call Bush derogatory names, they say, "But he's stupid." Being respectful and treating people, the way you'd like to be treated isn't about, "It's okay to have poor behavior" when it's someone you don't like. This is hypocritical behavior and I hear this kind of talk a lot from so called Godly and spiritual people. They become the very essence of that which they claim to not like.

Chapter 30

Trump Pulls a Rabbit from a Hat

The Trump effect forces us to examine ourselves and what we say we want. For years Americans have asked, "Why can't we have honest politicians who say what they mean?" Trump may not be 100% honest because none of us are; however, he's about as raw as you'll get with politicians speaking publicly about how they think and feel.

Do we really mean, "Please be honest as long as you say what I want to hear?" This is a dishonest way of relating. Many people say they dislike Trump because of the way he says certain things. When our focus is only on "how" someone says something and not "the message," we're using the messenger's style of relating as an excuse to dismiss the message. Delivery is important; however, the message should be greater than the style it was spoken. The truth is, we're too fragile to hear the truth. I've been accused of being brutally honest when I felt I was just being honest. It's interesting that Trump is sensitive about people saying negative things about him; however, he surely can dish it ou!. He feels justified attacking others because he says he doesn't go after people until they attack him.

Like Sen. Marco Rubio, Hillary should've stayed in her lane and not tried to Trump the The Donald. I have some coworkers who can be outright rude to customers and they don't get complaints; however, if I said the same to my customers, I'd get complaint letters. I thought it was unbecoming of Hillary to try and be a "Trumpster" and say immature things about him. She had to go low because she couldn't brag about her 30-year political career because a lot of her time was given to the Clinton Foundation.

Trump made the election fun and exciting. More Americans are paid attention to politics on a grand new level that only a magician could orchestrate. Years ago, my spiritual teacher said I needed to be aware of what was happening in my world and my consciousness would expand by having an understanding of politics and all areas of life. Collectively our Pandora's Box lid has flipped open and bats, dragons and demons are flying! We have an opportunity to see the worst in Hillary, Trump and ourselves. Take a moment and honestly reflect and admit when you have been racist, discriminatory, sexist, biased and hypocritical. Your truth will set you free and it will also help you lessen anger, hate and resentment for Trump and Hillary and for those who disagree with you politically.

I am a mystic. I help people see and understand meanings in themselves, others and situations that aren't always visible to the physical eye. It makes me happy when people who were uncomfortable discussing politics tell me that after discussing politics with me they now enjoy it and find it entertaining. Some have admitted that they didn't see themselves as racist, bias, or sexist until I asked them to scan their own psyche for that which they don't like in Trump or Hillary. Trump, Hillary and everyone's behavior gives us opportunities to learn how to be or not be.

A friend said to me, "We can discuss politics for hours and we'd end up agreeing to disagree."

"Speak for yourself. I am politically independent because I want to hear what all sides have to say, and you just may change my political views," I said.

I am not attached to any one way of being, thinking or feeling. I enjoy chatting with people about politics who agree with me; however, I find it more stimulating to discuss politics with people who think politically different from me because they trigger me to see issues from different viewpoints and angles.

Another woman told me, "I don't own a television and I didn't have an interest in politics. However, after the way you discuss politics I am going to buy a television and start watching it. In the meantime, I am going to watch politics on the internet." That was a huge compliment. We were able to both share and express how we felt in an emotionally mature way. She'd been turned off about discussing politics because people would get angry.

When people get angry because your political views are different from theirs, they're showing their controlling, immature, selfish ways. Their inner five-year-old thinks their anger will scare you into thinking as they do. I'd rather have dinner alone rather than be in the company of these kinds of people because they aren't coming from a place of love. They make me feel as if I am wearing a strait jacket on my mouth. Expressing our emotions can be healthy when we allow them to come to the surface and pay attention to what they're really saying to us. We don't usually get angry about what someone says to us, we get angry because what they said triggered our old emotional wounds and needs that are tender and are crying out to be healed.

This election is like playing political chess. You can strategically decide what move you'd like to make that would encourage healing, compassion and understanding for those who think, feel and believe differently than you. I can tell people I watch CNN and MSNBC and they don't have a response. But Lawdy Miss Clawdy, let me mention I watch Fox. News. Let the games begin! "Fox? How can you watch that racist, lying station?"

"What did people on Fox say that was more terrible than the way people on CNN and MSNBC speak about President George W. Bush and Sarah Palin?" I asked.

"But they're stupid."

"Oh, I see, if you think someone is stupid, then it's okay to demean them."

This behavior usually comes from so called liberals and Democrats who are supposed to be for the freedoms and rights for all. These kinds of liberals are willing to give you your freedoms as long as your beliefs coincide with theirs. Some people think Obama has been the most publicly disrespected politician because he's black. I think George W. Bush and Sarah Palin win the trophies for the most publicly demeaned. Nancy Pelosi was speaking about Obama's healthcare bill that was 2,700 pages. "We have to pass the bill so that you can find out what's in it." Can you imagine Sarah Palin saying this? If she did, this would've been called one of the dumbest comments a politician publicly made.

If Sarah Palin or George W. Bush would've made Obama's gaffe when he was on the campaign trail in 2008, they would've literally had dunce hats placed on their heads. Obama said, "I've visited 57 states and one left to go."

Television host Bill Maher called Palin a "cunt" and a "dumb twit." MSNBC host Martin Bashir resigned after calling George W. Bush a world class idiot. I am not a fan of George W. Bush or Obama; however, I will respect the office of the presidency as I disagree with their politics.

I don't think we should cease discussing politics or any subjects because some adults want to behave emotionally like five-year-olds because you disagree with them. If problems arise with people you claim to love and care about because they disagree with you, there's an opportunity for you to find ways to elevate your respect for each other so you may have mature, adult conversations. Suppression isn't healthy and people don't feel free when they feel forced to not mention certain topics to you. Control is sometimes disguised as love.

I have an ex-boyfriend who didn't like Fox's host Bill O'Reilly. Whenever I watched "The O'Reilly Factor" he would become quiet and treat me coldly. He was jealous because I enjoyed watching O'Reilly and I thought he was a smart man. Without consciously thinking about it, I found myself not watching Fox. I would not allow myself to be in this kind of relationship with friends, relatives or lovers again because this is not love-based behavior.

Who and what have we become as a people when we find it necessary to unfriend someone on Facebook because they choose to support a different politician than we may choose? If someone unfriends you because you have different political views than theirs, you should get on your knees and give a prayer of thanks that they're gone, bye-bye! I invite anyone who has a problem with me being a Trump supporter to graciously unfriend me. I allow people who support Hillary, Trump or any candidate on my Facebook page as long as they are able to be respectable. It would be mind-numbing for me to only want to communicate or hear about politics in the exact manner as I see them. I find it interesting that many people only watch cable news stations that support their way of thinking. How boring!

Some religious and spiritual people say they don't get involved with or discuss politics because it has no place in religion or spirituality. Politics probably started in churches. A friend said, "I don't get involved with politics because Jesus didn't get involved in politics." Jesus directly challenged the political and religious powers of his day. These powers were the wealthy ruling classes of Judea; the Sadducees and Pharisees. I love it when people claim to not do something because they said Jesus didn't do it, yet they break other Bible laws like fornicating and committing adultery. Many hide behind what Jesus did or didn't do as an excuse for what they choose to do or not do.

Chapter 31

Legalize Discrimination

Donald Sterling was the former owner of the NBA Clippers team. He was treated harshly for making racist comments about black people. His girlfriend who is part black and Mexican released audio that she said was the voice of Sterling. After seeing a picture his girlfriend posted on Instagram with Magic Johnson, he said, "You can sleep with black people. You can bring them in; you can do whatever you want. The little I ask is not to promote it on that ... and not to bring them to my games. It bothers me that you want to broadcast that you're associating with black people. Do you have to?"

When speaking about former NBA Lakers player Magic Johnson, Sterling said, "He should be ashamed of himself. He acts so holy. He made love to every girl in every city in America and he got AIDS. I didn't criticize him. I could have. Is he an example to those children? Jews, when they get successful, they will help their people. Some African Americans, they don't want to help anyone."

Is it possible for someone to say something that's the truth and racist at the same time? Magic Johnson has done a lot to help black people and he owns many black businesses that give people in the black community jobs. However, I agree with Sterling when he says that Jewish people tend to help their own more than black people do. This isn't racist, this is the truth. One of the biggest problems with black people is that we don't stick together and support each other. You rarely see and hear about Asian people protesting and crying racism because they're too busy becoming educated and being successful. Asian people and all races have experienced discrimination. Asians recognize the opportunities in America. Asian people don't have to start a movement that says, "Asian Lives Matter" because they show us how they matter because of how they live their lives and how they support each other. For the same reasons, Jewish people don't have to tell us, "Jewish Lives Matter." If Asians, Jewish people and any other races killed each other more than other races killed them, I wouldn't believe they believed their lives mattered. Show us your life matters!

Sterling was banned from the NBA, he can't own a team or attend an NBA game. I think this treatment was extreme given that he has the same feelings as many owners of professional teams. Sterling got caught. Many black people are racist and they express their anger when their friends and relatives date and marry white people. I think Sterling should've been allowed to keep his team as long as he paid his players properly and they were treated well. His personal feelings about a race shouldn't determine whether he can own a team or not. If the law said you can't have personal racist views and own a business or a sports team, there would be few business owners in America. Some of the same people who ostracized Sterling and said we shouldn't associate with racists wouldn't cease relationships with their relatives and personal friends who are racists. Many hypocritical people put Sterling down when they have the same beliefs about black people that he has.

Former Congressman Tom Tancredo, who is against illegal immigration, was ridiculed in the media because he said Miami looked like a third-world country. I agreed with Tancredo. I am from Miami and there are parts of Miami that I don't recognize anymore and I feel like I am in a foreign country when I visit. Someone said if Tancredo meant Miami looked like a third-world country because of the race of the people, then that makes his comment racist. I think the condition of a place and the behavior of the people is what makes it look like a third-world country. I have a friend who is Cuban who lives in California. She and her family recently visited Miami and her fourteen-year-old daughter asked her if the stores accepted American dollar bills because many people spoke foreign languages.

I think discrimination should be legal because it would make us more of an honest society. If we are a free country, we should be able to hire and fire anyone if we own a private company. The federal government shouldn't discriminate; however, private business owners should be able to hire and fire who they choose. Sometimes discrimination is necessary. If there were black petite women who were robbing banks and the police stopped me because I fit that description, I wouldn't think being questioned is racist.

Years ago, I went to an upscale shoe store in Coconut Grove, Florida with my three nieces. The white female clerk in the store gave us nasty looks and she watched us like a hawk. There was a pair of shoes I wanted, however, I didn't buy them because of the way the clerk treated us. A few days later, I contacted the store owner to complain about the treatment we received. The owner apologized for the clerk's behavior and said there had been groups of black females coming into the store grabbing shoes and running out. Though I didn't appreciate how I was treated, I understood why I got treated poorly. Because of the actions from my own people, I was mistreated. A lot of what black people complain about is a result of their own behavior.

I have been served discrimination more than I have ever received in my life because I am a Trump supporter. I've had people refuse to do work for me. I've had web designers, photographers and marketers refuse to help me with my books and speeches because they didn't want anything to do with Trump. I told these people, "You say you don't like Trump because he discriminates, however, you're discriminating against me." I also told them, "I am not asking you for a Trump endorsement, I am asking for technical help." I've received discrimination, because of Trump, from religious and metaphysical people who claim to be good and who champion for the rights for all. They are hypocrites. They champion for the rights of all people as long as "all" agree with them.

Liberals and Democrats who are black are astonished that I am a Trump supporter when the only reason they say they vote Democrat is, "Republicans are racist" or "I'm a Democrat because my great, great, great-grandparents were Democrats." I've heard the majority of black people I know make racist comments. How can we call the Tea Party members racist and not call members of Black Lives Matter racist? I don't think there's a human who hasn't thought or said something racist.

The same liberals who refused to do work for me because of Trump are some of the same people who felt the owner of the bakery in Lakewood, Colorado should've made the wedding cake for the same-sex couple. The owner of the bakery said he wouldn't make a cake for a pedophile or a same-sex couple because of his religion. The couple who was refused the cake said the treatment was offensive and dehumanizing. The judge ruled that the bakery owner was unlawful and discriminated against a gay couple by refusing to sell them a wedding cake. I was offended by the self-righteousness I got from people who refused to work for me because of Trump.

A young woman who was turning 18 was excited about being able to vote for the 2016 election. She went to an Albertson's supermarket to get a birthday cake made. She wanted, "Trump 2016" put on the cake. The baker refused to make the cake for her. When the story went public, a spokesperson for Albertson's tried to clean up the baker's behavior by saying the baker misunderstood the training provided regarding copyright phrases, and that's the reason why the customer was misinformed. I doubt the so-called baker would've had a problem with a "Hillary 2016" cake decoration.

In the '70s, Trump was sued for not renting his apartment units to black people. Many Democrats who call Trump racist probably had the same practices in the past. If I owned property I would like to have the right to rent to whomever I wanted to, and I should have the right in a free country to deny renting to people based on religion, race, sex or any other reason I decide. If Americans had the right to discriminate, I think we would be a more honest society because wolves wouldn't have to disguise who they are by wearing sheep costumes. We would know who everyone truly is and we could decide what businesses we want to support. Some black people think black people were more successful and productive during segregation. During segregation, there were more black businesses because we had to rely on ourselves more. There are many Jewish businesses because Jewish people were discriminated against years ago in America and they knew the best way to thrive would be through ownership.

Hooters restaurant was known for women having large breasts. Lawsuits were filed against Hooters by women with small breasts because they couldn't get hired. A Hooters black waitress sued because she was told black waitresses couldn't have blond highlights in their hair. Men sued Hooters because they didn't hire men as waiters. I think Hooters should be allowed to have these discriminations. If we were able to legally discriminate, I think people who didn't like the way companies discriminate would start companies that were all-inclusive. This way, we the people would be able to support people who discriminated or not and we wouldn't feel forced to be someone or something that we aren't. If we had legalized discrimination, there would be more authentic people in America.

Many liberals and Democrats remind me of some religious people. They are quick to call other people judgmental, however I find religious people to be some of the most judgmental people I've met. Liberals and Democrats claim to want rights, justice and freedoms for all, yet they're the ones who are stealing Trump signs from people's yards, denying services for people who are Trump supporters, they physically attack Trump supporters for wearing Make America Great Again hats, and they attack Trump supporters at his rallies. There have been Trump supporters who have attacked non-Trump supporters at rallies too; however, the most demonization is when you support Trump.

My Republican and conservative coworkers treat the janitors with more respect than my liberal, Democrat coworkers do. They speak to them and thank them for cleaning the office more often than my Democrat coworkers. I've mentioned this to my coworkers and they often agree. When you hear a traveling executive chewing out the van driver and hotel staff for things that are out of their control, they're usually a Democrat.

Buddhists behave the way Christians claim they are. Liberals and Democrats behave in ways that they accuse racist Republicans of behaving. I don't think you're a good person because you say you're for poor people and underdogs when you only feel this way when the poor and underdogs agree with your rhetoric.

Chapter 32

White Chocolate Wears Braids

Diamond and Silk are two sisters who support Trump. Because they're black, they get backlash from many black people for being Trumpettes. A black man told me, "I think Trump's campaign hired them to support him."

"I'm a Trump supporter. Do you think I was paid, too?"

"No. I don't think that about you because you speak in an intelligent way. White people like to see black people act ignorant like Diamond and Silk."

There is no style of communicating and relating that's acceptable to black people if you support a Republican. I don't think everyone must have the same style in order to be effective and entertaining. Many people pay attention to politics when people express it in a fun style the way Diamond and Silk does. Black people who don't like Diamond and Silk have more complaints about them than they do black gang bangers who kill black people.

Some white people don't think black women should have blond hair. Some black women are offended when they hear this, yet they want to have the right to wear braids all to themselves. A white man was grabbed and pushed by a black woman at San Francisco State University because his hair was dreaded. The white man asked the woman, "You're saying I can't have a hair style because of your culture? Why?"

"Because it's my culture." She accused him of appropriating her culture.

Some black women think it's a slap in their face for white women to wear braids. Black people don't own the rights to the word nigger, and we don't own the rights to dreads and braids. I find it to be complimentary for people to want to imitate things my race does. I enjoy learning about new styles and ways of doing things from other races and cultures. In 1979, Bo Derek starred in the movie "10" wearing cornrow braids. Black women were pissed off because the media had ignored black women wearing braids and suggested that Derek was the one who invented braids. Bo Derek wearing braids made more white people pay attention to black women's creative hair styles, so I felt that was a positive.

Sometimes, black people get too angry when they should see other races wanting to mimic their style as a compliment. We all take a bit of our style and creations from others. I wasn't offended when dancer Julianne Hough, who is white, wore a Halloween costume in the likeness of a black female character from the television show "Orange Is the New Black." She wore an orange prison jumpsuit, had her hair in individual hair knots and her face was made up in black face. There was an outrage on social media and on news outlets. Hough was mimicking a character and she wanted to look realistic. It's possible that sometimes people are admiring who we are and not putting us down by copying our style. Because Hough had black face didn't mean she was demeaning people with black skin. It was a costume!

The Native American Indian culture is one of my favorite because I like the way they made use of what they had and they didn't believe in waste. I like the way they honored and respected animals even though they killed them for food and clothing. They selected the weakest animal to kill first and when they died, their bodies were put in the wilderness for the animals to partake of. I love Indian feather headdresses, and if I wore one as a costume it would be out of admiration for the Indian culture. If I wore a China doll costume I would like to wear white powdered makeup on my face to look like an authentic China doll. My purpose would be to imitate, not demean. One of the reasons we have so many problems is because we take ourselves way too seriously. We should see the beauty and fun in someone mimicking who and what we are with our costumes. We really need to be able to laugh at ourselves more.

Years ago, I saw a white man at a Halloween party wearing a gigantic afro. He had black makeup on his face and he wore a large gold chain necklace with a large slice of watermelon that was made from plastic attached to it. Black people, white people and other race people were at the party and no one was offended. We thought he was creative and he made us laugh because we knew white people liked watermelon and chicken just as much as black people do!

Actor Tom Hanks' son, Chet Haze, who is also known as "White Chocolate," is a rapper and he's down with hanging out with the brothers. He has gotten criticized for saying the word nigga. He said, "No one can tell me I can't say nigga. Hip-hop and rap isn't about race, it's actually extremely fresh that I say nigga. Nigga unifies the culture of hip-hop across all races, which is actually kind of a beautiful thing. Camaraderie and love—not just exclusively for black people." I agree with White Chocolate saying he too should have the right to say the word nigger.

I am not into censorship of any words because I'm a writer and author. Censoring words suppresses expression. Every word has its proper place. Just because White Chocolate was raised by his rich actor parents doesn't mean his spirit doesn't identify with black rappers. When I see White Chocolate, and watch him speak and rap, I think maybe he's the incarnation of a black rapper.

Chapter 33

How I Made Racism Disappear

We have become some world these days. People who have bad behavior are now holding our politicians' hostage. Illegal immigrants cross our borders illegally and start their lives in America, and politicians who want them to return to their native countries become the racist boogeymen. Black Lives Matter members chant in the streets they want cops harmed, yet our politicians have to be very careful how they respond to their remarks because they don't want to be called racist.

Every group has their privilege. All races are killed by police, however it's the killings of the black men by white police officers that make the news. Any ethnic group can shout racism however no one's voice is as loud as the African Americans. This will always be the case, because black people were slaves in America. We all have different experiences; however, I didn't have the racist experiences that many black people say they've had. This doesn't mean that people aren't racist toward me, but rather my focus is towards improving my life on a daily basis so I don't see overt racism toward me. Some black people say racism is the biggest problem in their lives. I was the biggest problem in my life. When I recognized that, I started making major changes in my life and I had sessions with professional therapists to help me reprogram my belief system.

Motivational, inspirational and transformational speakers can and are making a big difference in our world. I was able to make major changes in my life by attending courses given by these kinds of speakers. Les Brown, T. Harv Eker, Robert Kiyosaki, Tony Robbins and Dr. John Demartini. These courses aren't about how to remain victims, the focus is about showing you how you can live your greatness. When I focused on my own issues, I lost track of what wasn't going right in my life because of what someone else did to me because I was too busy taking my power back. I learned from these teachers that I had the power to change whatever I didn't like about my life. These teachers' and speakers' messages are far from the message you get from the Democratic Party, who teach and perpetuate your life is dim because of racism and the Republicans. These teachers teach you that you can be wealthy, healthy and successful regardless of your race or gender if you're willing to do the necessary work, educate yourself on your craft and become disciplined. These kinds of courses and seminars would be valuable for young people to attend before deciding on spending thousands of dollars on college because they can get clarity on who and what they are.

Black people condemn other black people who are conservatives. Some think black conservatives are the problem with black people because they call black people who want to be criminals, blame their problems on white people, not work and refuse to get educated victims. Black people who kill, riot, loot, and burn the cities they live in dislike black Republicans. It's black privilege to have people in the media and politicians make excuses for this outrageous behavior. If more black people were Republicans there would be more successful black people and more black people would be alive.

Black actress "Monique" boarded a commercial airplane for a flight. She sat in first class and her entourage was seated in the back. Her hair dresser came to first class to put her hair dryer in the overhead bin. A white male flight attendant approached the hairdresser about where he placed the hair dryer. "Monique" felt the flight attendant was rude and disrespectful to her employee and she got into an argument with him.

"Monique" and her staff were thrown off the plane and they took a later flight. She said the experience was humiliating and that this happens to black people all the time. She considered filing a lawsuit and she publicly encouraged black people not to fly on the airline. I am a frequent flyer and I can tell you that these kinds of situations happen daily on airplanes with all race people. This doesn't mean that some of the experiences aren't based on racism; however, often it's poor behavior colliding. "Monique" would've gotten more support if she asked people of all races to boycott the airline based on poor, rude customer service rather than making it about racism.

Black people are the only race that condemns their own people for not politically voting the way they think they should vote because of their skin color. Black Lives Matter should be protesting outside the White House because they have a sitting black president who hasn't helped them improve conditions in black communities. Obama was more focused on spending his time helping hundreds of thousands of Syrians get legal status in America and he wanted to help illegal immigrants get legal status so they can hopefully pad votes for the Democratic Party. Obama had already sealed the black community vote, so they weren't a priority.

There was a recent riot in North Carolina because a black man was killed by a black police officer. If Dr. Martin Luther King was alive, he would've taken his megaphone and gone into the city and talked to the people and encouraged them to protest nonviolently and he would've given them legitimate reasons as to why rioting, looting and violently attacking innocent people isn't the way to create healing and change. Some black people like the attention they get from rioting when a black person is killed by police because it gives them a false sense that their lives are valued more when a white person takes their life. The media loves seeing black people act like packs of wild savages burning their own communities. They burn their already dilapidated neighborhoods instead of burning rich white peoples' (who they claim they're angry with) neighborhoods. They know prolonged destruction and rioting in white neighborhoods by black people wouldn't be tolerated on the levels that it is in poor neighborhoods.

Cam Newton is the quarterback for the Carolina Panthers. In speaking about the riot in North Carolina, he said, "I'm African American, I'm not happy what or how justice has been dealt with over the years, the state of oppression in our community. But we also, as black people, have to do right by ourselves. We can't be hypocrites." Cam said the magic word, "hypocrites." The daily oppression that's occurring in many black inner cities is coming from black people killing, attacking, stealing, and raping each other.

When I was a police officer in Miami, Dr. Martin Luther King Jr.'s birthday celebration was one of the highest crime days in the city. It was shameful to see and feel so much oppression from my own people on the day we were supposed to celebrate the man's birthday who was about freedom and uplifting for all races of people with shootings, stabbings and robberies. A day that was supposed to be celebratory in the black community became an embarrassment for some black police officers.

When black people rioted and protested in Ferguson, Missouri and Baltimore, Maryland, Obama didn't do what King would've done. Obama has done a sorry job when it comes to healing racial tensions in America. It's strange how Obama had passive comments when we are attacked by Islamic terrorists, have riots in inner cities and black people shoot, kill, and are violent with each other in Chicago and other inner cities. My friend Denise would say, "Girl, something smells fishy and it ain't me because I showered." Maybe Obama's passivity about these situations has to do with him wanting things to be out of control in America, so he can justify America is a racist nation. Maybe when Americans were attacked in terrorist attacks by Islamic terrorists, he felt like his former pastor Reverend Wright, who said this about 9/11, "America's chickens have come home to roost."

Boxing promoter Don King caught holy hell for publicly endorsing Trump. Celebrities took to Twitter to slam him. Rapper T.I. called King a spineless soul-selling coon Negro, poor excuse for a black man for selling your own people out, fucking disgrace and a stupid ass. Actress Vivica A. Fox tweeted, "You are a complete embarrassment to black people." Rapper 50 Cent put a prayer on Instagram, "Let us pray Lord, please don't let Trump into office. We will spin out of control." Truth is, we're already out of control and I think Trump is the best to bring us back into balance. No black person or any other person using their right to vote is selling me out because of their personal choice to vote for whomever they choose.

Don King voted for Obama in 2008 and 2012. In 1966, King killed two men. He got off on justifiable homicide on one of the killings, and the other charge was reduced to manslaughter. He served over three years in prison and eventually received a full pardon. The media is going wild reporting his past criminal charges; however, they didn't try to smear him when he endorsed Obama. Black celebrities speak harshly of famous black people who vote for Trump because they want to intimidate other blacks out of supporting him. For this reason, some black celebrities are afraid to publicly support Trump.

Writer Drew Magary wrote an article in a GQ (Gentlemen Quarterly) magazine that was entitled "Fuck Ben Carson." Can you imagine a writer publicly saying the same about Obama? If he did, there would've been a boycott to get rid of GQ. Magary is a white man and he, too, knows it's safe to beat up on a black man in America if he's a Republican. Black Democrats didn't run to Carson's defense; however, there would've been a stampede if this was done to Obama. I am about free speech, but I didn't appreciate Magary doing this to my brother because I know he wouldn't have done the same about a black male Democrat. He did it because he knows the oppression black people lay on their own who are Republicans.

Black people call actress Stacey Dash, and reality game show personality Omarosa Manigault, "Tomasina's," and neurosurgeon Ben Carson and radio talk show host Larry Elder are called "Uncle Toms" for supporting Trump. Some black websites call Dash the most hated black person because in 2012, she publicly said she was voting for Mitt Romney. You'd think the most hated black people in America would be the black gang bangers that are assaulting and killing black people. Al Sharpton and Jesse Jackson only come to the rescue of a black person who is publicly demeaned when they're a Democrat. A black woman told me she didn't like Dash because she said black people can be successful if they work hard. I agreed with Dash. The woman who dislikes Dash for saying this took out student loans and worked and paid her way through college. Just as she was able to accomplish this, all black people today in America have the same opportunity.

I have white friends who say it's puzzling to them when black successful people make excuses for black people who want to be career criminals and blame the white man for their problems, because they think if their black friends were able to create successful lives for themselves, they should realize all black people have the same opportunities.

The only oppression I have felt has come from black people. During my early school years, I was an "A" student. I was called a white girl because I was smart and I wanted to learn to play the piano and ride horses. Some black male gang bangers are geniuses and smart men; however, they get teased and put down from their own community so they choose to be criminals to fit in. This is evil to do to someone, yet black people only want to see the ills white people cause them.

There's a lot of oppression in the black community because of the black on black crime and drug use. There are some good people who live in poor black communities; however, their own people oppress them more than any white man. When I hear black people criticize their own people for having different political views than they have, it makes me feel like they're taking the place of the white slave master and they're trying to control how black people feel and think in the same way the white slave master treated us. Black people keep alive what they say they don't like. My consciousness isn't dictated by the color of my skin. My experiences shape who I am and I appreciate my right to vote for whomever I choose, just as I give others their rights.

Chapter 34

Oscar Madness

Just because someone says something is racist, doesn't mean it's racist. The new definition of racism is, "I disagree with you." Actress Jada Pinkett Smith, who is married to actor Will Smith, boycotted the Oscars because she said it's racist and lacks diversity. Some people felt she was angry because her husband wasn't nominated for best actor in the movie "Concussion." I haven't seen the movie, however I've heard people say the Nigerian accent Will Smith used was poor and his acting was just okay. Leonardo DiCaprio got an Oscar for best actor in the movie "Revenant," his only other Academy Award nomination was 22 years prior. It took years for Denzel Washington to get an Oscar. Over the years when people asked Denzel how it felt to not have received an Oscar, he would say his work speaks for itself. He's absolutely correct. Denzel and Leonardo are much better actors than Will Smith—his acting is mediocre.

Janet Hubert was an actress on the show "The Fresh Prince of Bel Air." She spoke out about Jada asking other black actors and actresses to boycott the Oscars. "There's a lot of shit going on in the world that you all don't seem to recognize. People are dying. Our boys are being shot left and right. People are starving. People are trying to pay bills. And you're talking about motherfucking actors and Oscars. It just ain't that deep. I find it ironic that somebody who has made their living and made millions and millions of dollars from the very people you're talking about boycotting just because you didn't get a nomination, just because you didn't win." I love what Hubert said and I agreed with her.

There are also white actors who are snubbed at award shows, but they don't cry racism. It's possible the Academy judges don't like your movie and your acting and it's possible the race of an actor may not be the reason they weren't given an award. Moving forward, the Academy may give black people Oscars just to say they're not being racist. This is reverse racism, when someone who is a better actor is snubbed for political correctness. Maybe it would've been a good idea to meet with the Oscar judges and get their feedback as to why they didn't vote for certain movies. Diversity has gone wild! As a result, we aren't getting the best talent or the best person for the job. Some talk shows try to have hosts that are black, white, Asian, Latino and other races. However, often these people aren't talented and their race isn't enough to pad their generic performances. I would rather have a panel of all white, all black, all Asian, all Latino or all whatever race of talented people, rather than having lame talent or people getting jobs based on their race just for the sake of showing diversity.

Monica Lewinsky is still treated like a leper by many people because of her affair with Bill Clinton when he was president. Bill Clinton is still held in high regard by the same people who demonize Lewinsky. Some think that what happened was Lewinsky's fault. Women are some of the biggest offenders of speaking harshly about her. Lewinsky did a Ted Talk speech that I felt was outstanding. I think she's been punished long enough.

I am surprised that in 2016 students at universities are still allowed to shout down speakers who disagree with them. I think this is allowed because liberal professors enjoy the students agreeing with their views. Students are being shortchanged by not being able to listen to people who think, feel and see differently. Liberal universities put down racist Republicans for not accepting homosexuality and abortions; however, they're just as guilty of suppression of people's rights when speakers are shouted down and aren't allowed to express their views. Liberal universities are more careful with putting Muslims down about their beliefs on homosexuality and abortions. This is shameful, and professors who condone or encourage students to do this should be fired because they're trying to silence free thought. This is dictator-like behavior to only allow people to speak if they agree with you. Hitler wanted to silence free thought, too.

A white coworker told me she went to see the movie "Soul Plane." The movie is a comedy about an airline that's owned and run by black ghetto people. My white coworker told a black coworker, "I went to see the movie 'Soul Plane' last night, it was really funny."

"I want you to know what you just said was racist," the black coworker said. My white coworker was confused and didn't understand why watching a black comedy movie was racist. Maybe the black coworker felt that only black people can watch black movies just as some of my people think only black people have the rights to the word nigger.

I don't think we should skinny shame or fat shame. You get a pass from the political correct police if you skinny shame; however, you're put in disgrace jail if you say something negative about fat people. Actress Gabourey Sidibe is a black actress. She's five feet five inches tall and she weighs hundreds of pounds. People on talk shows often speak about actresses who are too skinny and look anorexic. Some people publicly say these thin women are poor role models for young women, however, they won't say the same about Sidibe. When Sidibe is on talk shows, it's obvious the host is noticing her weight, but they wouldn't dare mention it out of fear of the politically correct police shouting racism, fat shaming and discrimination because she's black and obese.

France passed a law that banned excessively thin models. People who hire excessively thin models can be fined and go to jail. Imagine the worldwide outcry if there was a ban prohibiting obese women from being models. This would be called discriminatory and shallow. Anorexia and obesity are extremes and both are unhealthy; however, you can only publicly speak negatively about the thin extreme. When I was young, I was skinny and I was teased often. My fat cousin said I had skinny toothpick legs and I called her fat buffalo butt. She told her mother what I said and my mother spanked me and said, "You aren't supposed to call people fat." My mother knew my cousin called me offensive names because I was skinny but it didn't matter. At a young age, I became aware of this double standard, my hurt feelings didn't matter to others because I was skinny.

Chapter 35

The End Zone

A friend told me that her pastor said we are in trouble because Trump may become president. I don't think we're in trouble because Trump or Hillary could become president. I think we're in trouble because of who we the people are. We are serial hypocrites who lack integrity and authenticity, yet we want our leaders to be something we are not. Our leaders are a representation of who we are. Our leaders can't lead us to the promised land when we bash them for speaking their truths when we disagree with them. We are demanding our leaders remain fake as long as they appease what we believe.

   Some say Trump's ego is gigantic and he's called a narcissist. I think Obama is also a narcissist, egomaniac, and it's all about him. Obama recently publicly said, "Don't insult me by not voting for Hillary." He also said, "I will consider it a personal insult to my 'legacy' if you don't vote for Hillary." Trump would publicly be called a selfish egomaniac if he said the same. If Trump is elected, Obama is afraid Trump may be a successful president by undoing some of his policies and he thinks that would affect his legacy.

   Iyanla Vanzant is a black woman. She's a lawyer, inspirational speaker, author, and life coach. She has a show called, "Iyanla Fix My Life." She does an awesome job in helping people evolve from a life of being a victim because of what happened to them in the past. She said she was called a nigger by white adults when she was young, however that didn't' have anything to do with who she is today. This is because she made a decision to not let what happened to her in her past paralyze her. By educating herself and learning life lessons, she became a successful black woman.

I had a spiritual teacher tell me not to take my past into my future and to focus on the mystery in my life rather than the history. Focusing on the history kept me in the past, while focusing on the mystery keeps me in the present as I ponder and wonder what the meaning of what was happening to me daily meant. I learned that what I *did* with what happened to me was more important than *what* happened to me. Years ago, I was blessed to be a part of a government program called CETA (Comprehensive Employment and Training Act) that paid salaries for minorities to companies that didn't have budget funds to hire more employees. My first job through CETA was training to become a dispatcher for the police department. A few years later, I got hired as a police officer. I probably wouldn't have become a police officer if I didn't have the experience of being a police dispatcher.

The CETA program was run poorly. There were black people hanging out on street corners and not going to their job assignments while they collected checks from the government. For this reason, some critics said the CETA program wasn't effective. The problem was the lack of management of the program. Government employees didn't pay attention to the program and minorities weren't held responsible for not showing up for work. I made the program work for me because I was responsible. I was appreciative to have been chosen to be part of the program and I wanted to make good on my opportunity.

I met a white medical doctor who told me he had an experience with CETA, too. He said he'd wanted to be a fireman since he was a young boy. Because of the CETA program, the fire department had to give minorities the fire academy positions. Instead of being angry with minorities for the rest of his life, he went to medical school and became a doctor. This is a fine example of *what* you do with *what* happens to you.

One of the problems in our world today is the lack of gratitude. When I first went to my therapist, she said, "Show me an unhappy person and I will see a person who lacks gratitude." I thought I was a thankful person, however I realized I needed to increase my gratitude level. Writing out ten things daily that I am thankful and grateful for reminds me of the many blessings I have, and it keeps me focusing on what is working and what I do have rather than what I don't have and what's not working. My life flows gently now and I am constantly blessed as long as my gratitude meter is high.

America isn't perfect; however, we Americans still have a lot to be thankful for. When I see flight attendants, waiters and waitresses serve people, I rarely hear "thank you." When I fly in first class, my fellow passengers only speak to the flight attendants when they want to order something. The flight attendant asks the passenger, "Would you care for something to drink?"

"Coke."

You rarely hear, "May I please have a coke, or coke please." Customers rarely say "thank you" when they're served or the flight attendants and waiters pick up their trash and dishes. The other side of the coin are the rude, ungrateful employees. The death of manners in America and our world creates a toxic, greedy, selfish, ungrateful energy. We are not being gracious and appreciating one another. We must also be gracious to one another by accepting others may have different political views.

New Yorkers can be difficult passengers. My flight attendant friend told me about an incident in Hawaii. An airplane that was to fly from Hawaii to Newark had a broken landing gear. The passengers were angry because the plane was broken and there was nearly a riot at the gate. The customer service agent had to call the police. I find it bizarre that people get angry about not being able to fly in broken airplanes. I understand customers can be upset about airlines having problems often, however, regardless of how often mechanics are aware that a plane needs to repaired, I am thankful they are aware of the problems. If the passengers focused on being thankful for being safe, their anger would dissolve because being safe is what's important.

People who constantly bitch about the conditions of the airlines shouldn't fly. Folks say they have to fly because of their jobs. There are always choices, and we can choose to have jobs where we don't have to travel on planes.

A lot of the chaos and tension in America and our world has to do with personal dissatisfaction. It's a fad to blame someone else for your poor-quality life that's really a result of the poor choices you've made. There's little to no effort for unhappy people to make necessary changes in their lives, because change takes work and healthy habits take discipline and commitment. In order to have healthy habits, you have to remove toxic people, places, things, and environments from your life and many aren't willing to do this.

Racism hasn't stopped me from having any job that I've wanted. I think I have had more opportunities because I am a black woman. I am able to discuss illegal immigration and get away with it much easier than white people can. A woman asked me, "If you're so spiritual, why do you give energy to illegal immigration?"

I explained to her that illegal immigration that causes demise of poor American citizens isn't a good thing, and I discuss it because spiritually it's wrong for politicians to cause harm to their own people for the sake of pimping illegal immigrants for Electoral College votes. The spirit and the energy of politicians doing this is a dark energy. Some people think that being a spiritual person means you're nice and you reward poor behavior.

The era of everybody gets a trophy doesn't help people to be responsible and understand that life isn't always equal and that your input in life determines your output. This output shouldn't be the responsibility for someone else to carry you. Capitalism (an economic political system in which a country's trade and industry are controlled by private owners for profit, rather than by state) is beautiful because you're rewarded for your efforts through money and it helps you to have creative ideas and be innovative.

I would like for Trump to win. Regardless of who becomes president, I am going to continue to be blessed as long as I am willing to take responsibility for my own choices. We will get whatever lessons we need as a people regardless of who becomes president. I am excited about the changes this election has created.

When black people riot, loot, kill their own and commit a high number of crimes, other races don't respect them. White people and other races are skeptical about what is readily called wrongful police shootings of black men when they later hear about the dead black person's extensive past criminal record. There's a dark, violent energy in many poor black neighborhoods and this energy attracts more darkness and violence. This would also cause more conflicts with the police. There are less conflicts when the environments are peaceful.

By no means am I justifying someone being killed because they have a long felony criminal record. Whether someone has a criminal record or not, there should be prosecution for the police, or anyone, who takes someone's life unlawfully. What I am saying is that black people will have to first calm the tensions in their own communities before others, including the police, can come in and create change. If black people believed the chant, "Black Lives Matter," their neighborhoods wouldn't be riddled with massive crime. I know what's possible because of the changes I've made in my life. I have a totally different life because I was willing to focus on my own personal issues and stop blaming others for the outcome of my poor choices.

I look forward to working with people in the black community to help them recognize the inner power they posess. Drug use and alcohol abuse are poor choices that equals poor results. There would be a drastic drop in crime and police shootings in black communities if they focused first individually and as a group to get healthy and clean in mind, body and, spirit. There are some good, clean and decent black people who feel trapped in the crime-ridden inner cities. More black people would forget about racism if they made inner positive changes within themselves. Racism will naturally dissipate when a community becomes healthy and whole because they will attract different experiences. Racism may not disappear in the world, however it surely can in your personal world.

My soon-to-be-released memoir, "Buy Your Own Damn Cocktail" is a story about how I made the woes in my life disappear. What I used to call problems are just invitations for me to have opportunities to grow. Black women have a natural strength and power. I am a proud black woman, and I think it's an honor to be one regardless of the "isms" that will always exist. If I was reincarnated, I'd want to be a black woman again!

I encourage you to daily give thanks and gratitude for at least 10 things. There's a hand/heart connection that makes writing out daily your list of ten things you're grateful for powerful. You will see your life change and negative experiences will fade. When negative experiences appear, ask what they are supposed to teach you and raise your gratitude energy. If black people and every race was committed to being the best they could be every day, we would be a happier, more peaceful and productive world.

I feel the biggest problem in our world isn't because of the politicians' that we have. Lack of gratitude is the biggest problem we face. Gratitude is love based, magical and healing. Gratitude puts you in the face of God. I highly recommend you read the book, "Don't Sweat the Small Stuff—and it's all small stuff" by Richard Carlson. I have read this book about four times and I keep it in my bathroom and I read a page daily to remind me to not, "sweat the small stuff." This small, yet powerful book changed my life and helped me to be healthier, have less stress and have more gratitude and appreciation for my life.

Zendaya is a bi-racial actress. She's gotten negative feedback from some black people because they don't think she owns up to the part of her that's black. She and a friend went to a supermarket to buy $400 worth of gift cards. She said the clerk refused to sell her the gift cards because of her skin color. She alleges the clerk told her she couldn't afford the gift cards and tossed her wallet. On social media, she posted, "This is what we deal with." Her male friend piped in and said, "Because we're black." Maybe this story helped Zendaya get more street cred with some black people. I wondered how she automatically knew the clerk discriminated against her because of her skin color. What if the clerk was just a jerk and unprofessional, or had some other kind of psychological problems, or what if the clerk was triggered to be rude because of the behavior of Zendaya and her friend? I don't know, I wasn't there; however, I think a lot of what we call racism isn't racism.

If we don't like racism, we must also be willing to not readily call situations and people racist when the problem or behavior may not be racist. The word racism has been minimized because it's used frivolously. Pay attention to situations when people of the same race treat each other poorly, yet when someone of a different race behaves the same way, it's automatically called racism. This is hypocritical behavior and it fuels the racism volcano. Don't be a part of what you say you hate. We need to first get right with ourselves before we can heal the world.

Though I would like to have Trump win the 2016 presidency, my crystal ball doesn't tell me who will win though my divine messages often tell me he will win. However, today I think the momentum is in Trump's favor and if he learns his karmic lessons of learning to listen to wisdom from others and knowing when to silence his ego, he will win. I am excited about the changes Trump has brought to the election process. The presidential election will never be the same, regardless of who wins. I am not attached to the outcome of the election. Whether Trump or Hillary wins, I will continue to count my many daily blessings and continue to live my best life and I celebrate and give thanks to be an American!

Before you call Trump a racist, be honest with yourself and remember the racist thoughts, words, feelings, and poor behaviors you have. Before you call Hillary a liar, remember all the lies you've told, even the so called white lies. A lie is a lie, even if it's about Santa Claus and the Tooth Fairy.

About the Author

Ce Ce Ferrari, America's Hottest Thought Provoking Speaker is a Transformational Speaker and author who has a dynamic way of speaking and relating. She's an expert at helping people connect with their hidden emotions and she teaches the power of taking personal responsibility. She's a former Miami Metro Dade Police Officer and Megawatt-Radio Personality. Her views on politics and Black Lives Matter are deeply rooted from her experiences from working the mean streets of Miami as a cop. She worked patrol and undercover. She has helped many people transform their lives by helping them understand that everything that happens to us is a gift and an opportunity for us to create a change or learn something new. Her next soon to be released book is her memoir, "Buy Your Own Damn Cocktail."

Visit **CeCeFerrari.com** to hire Ce Ce for speaking engagements and for updates on her upcoming books, blogs and fun free stuff!

Ce Ce Ferrari

www.ingramcontent.com/pod-product-compliance
Lightning Source LLC
Chambersburg PA
CBHW060845280326
41934CB00007B/924